THE LANGUAGE OF BASEBALL:

A Complete Dictionary of Slang Terms, Clichés, and Expressions from the Grand Ole Game

Ryan Gray

ISBN: 1-58518-628-7

Book layout: Jennifer Bokelmann
Cover design: Larry Wood
Cartoon illustrations: Daniel Brown
Cover photo: Carla Rafferty

Coaches Choice
P.O. Box 1828
Monterey, CA 93942
www.coacheschoice.com

Throughout this book, the masculine shall be deemed to include the feminine and vice versa.

FOREWORD

The game of baseball holds a special place in the hearts of millions of Americans. Perhaps it is because the "Great American Pastime", among all other sports, is most like real life. Baseball, like America, was founded on rugged individualism and a distinct set of never changing virtues. Within the American culture there is a baseball sub-culture with its own values and mores.

Since baseball's inception in the late 1800's, there has been an ever-expanding body of knowledge as well as an ever-increasing language. A unique dialect of slang and clichés exists that colorfully describe the goings on of baseball. Baseball-speak is children's banter on a sandlot, a grizzled fan yelling at an umpire, and the latest description for a great play on television and radio. All of the people surrounding the game communicate with their own language of baseball.

Ryan Gray's book, *The Language of Baseball*, contains descriptions of baseball terminology simple enough for a child to comprehend and yet sophisticated enough for the most knowledgeable fans. Within this book you will find definitions ranging from the historical and educational to the mechanical and strategic aspects of the game of baseball.

As you read this book, I'm sure you will find it both informative and fun.

Ron Polk
Head Baseball Coach
Mississippi State University

ACKNOWLEDGMENTS

First and foremost, to my Lord and Savior Jesus Christ from whom all wisdom flows – You died and rose that I may live.

To my loving wife Danica, for the encouragement, love, and sacrifice she has displayed through our life together.

To my daughters Reagan (4) and Rylee (1) for adding more love and joy to my life everyday.

To my parents, Ralph and Joan Gray, for the lifelong love and support they have shown in all my endeavors.

To my father Ralph Gray and my late grandfather, Shannon Gray, for passing down to me their passion for the game of baseball and especially their allegiance to the St. Louis Cardinals.

To Jack Buck and Mike Shannon for helping bolster my respect for baseball and the St. Louis Cardinals. What an inspiration it was to hear your daily explanations of strategies, your rich vocabulary of the game, and your contagious optimism while promoting the grand ole game.

To Ron Polk for writing the forward for this book.

To "Itch" Jones, Steve Peterson, and Mike Matheny for providing endorsements for this book.

To Daniel Brown for his time and effort in creating the cartoon illustrations for this book.

To Elliot Johnson for allowing me to use The Winning Run. May our Lord continue to bless you as you boldly proclaim the truth of the Gospel.

To the Coaching Baseball class: Garon, Henry, Javy, Mario, Muchacho, and Walt.

To Greg and Josh who were there when the idea for this book was conceived.

To Nick "The Stick" Hunter and Barry Weinberg.

CONTENTS

Baseball has always been one of the most important parts of my life. From my early years playing in the coach-pitch fish-league for the Eldorado Bluegills to my recent years coaching some future professionals, baseball has had a permanent influence on my life. Some of my earliest memories are of listening to the St. Louis Cardinals' radio broadcasts with my father and grandfather. Their love of baseball and the Cardinals was passed on to me in a very profound way.

I gained a lot of my knowledge regarding terms, strategies, and the history of the game from listening to Mike Shannon and Jack Buck on the radio. Even today, hearing their voices as they call a Cardinals' game still takes me back to the hot, sweltering, humid Southern Illinois summers of my childhood. I sincerely want my own and all children to grow up with a love for the game of baseball. I hope that this book will spark an interest in the casual observer and increase the interest of the avid fan.

I have always believed that you can tell a lot about people by the words they use. I find that words are a good indicator of a person's knowledge of baseball as well. For years I have been interested and fascinated by what people say about baseball. I have made a point of listening carefully and remembering the terms used by all of the people who spoke their own language of baseball.

A friend of mine, whose son was nine at the time, was talking to me about the humorous yet sometimes ignorant things that parents and coaches yell at youth players regarding techniques and strategies. After discussing some of them I told my friend that I ought to write a book on baseball slang and clichés. That was the beginning.

The first terms I wrote down and defined were "long strike", "straighten it out", and "bend yer back." I initially thought of naming this book "Bend Yer Back". Ever since I was young that cliché has amused me, as if bending your back was the cure-all that could fix all of the pitching woes for all of the young pitchers who couldn't throw strikes.

Most of the terms in this book are old "tried and true" expressions and clichés. However, some were coined as late as the 2001 baseball season. I hope that readers will find this information both fun and educational. I'm confident that this book will increase your baseball knowledge, and perhaps even affect how people perceive you. After all, some people can tell a lot about you by the words you use.

JUST FOR FUN

Throughout the text, 20 "quiz pictures" are randomly placed—each of which represent a slang baseball term found in this book. Take a moment to try and guess what each picture attempts to depict; then check your answers on page 107.

GOOD LUCK!

A. Abbreviation for assists.

A ball. The Class A level of minor league baseball.

AA ball. The Class AA level of minor league baseball.

AAA ball. The class AAA level of minor league baseball.

AAAA player. Expression for a player who is a decent AAA player but doesn't achieve enough success in the big leagues to stick; he is called up and sent down many times during his career.

AABC. American Amateur Baseball Congress; for players ages eight to adult.

AAU. Amateur Athletic Union; for players ages eight to eighteen.

AB. Abbreviation for at bats.

AB/HR. Abbreviation for the ratio of home runs per at bats.

AB/K. Abbreviation for the ratio of strikeouts per at bats.

ABCA. American Baseball Coaches Association; the premier baseball coaches association in the world.

a cancer in the clubhouse. Refers to a player who causes division on a team and helps to create bad team chemistry.

ace. Term for a team's best pitcher.

aches and pains. Refers to a player who is always complaining about having nagging injuries.

acquisition. When a team obtains the services of a player, usually brought about by a trade or free agent signing.

action stance. A stance used by catchers when they must block every ball in the dirt, including the following situations: a) any runners on base, b) a three ball count, c) a two strike count, or d) a 3-2 count.

add insult to injury. Expression used when an opponent intentionally runs up the score against a team that is already losing badly.

advance scout. A professional scout who watches and takes notes on a team that his organization's team will soon play.

Advanced A. The highest level of Class A ball in minor league baseball.

affair. Term for a baseball game.

affiliate. A minor league franchise associated with a major league baseball franchise.

"A" game. When a player is playing at his peak level of performance.

aggressive lead. Refers to a base runner's lead consisting of two hard shuffle steps.

airmail. Term for when a player overthrows his target.

albatross. Refers to a team that always gives another team a tough game.

ALCS. Abbreviation for the American League Championship Series.

ALDS. Abbreviation for the American League Division Series.

alibi Ike. Name for a player who constantly makes excuses.

"A" lick. When a batter hits a ball as far as he can hit it.

all bets are off. Phrase meaning that anything can happen.

alleys. Left-center and right-center field.

alligator the ball. A youth league term for a fielding technique on ground balls in which the inside part of both wrists remain touching. This contributes to a quicker release and provides a safety fac-

tor since a bounding ball will hit the palm of the fielder's hand instead of his face.

all out. Term for when a player gives his maximum effort.

aloha means goodbye. Phrase used by some announcers after a home run is hit.

also-ran. Term for a very bad player or team.

altercation. A fight between players on two opposing teams.

"American League" baseball. Term for a strategy where the major emphasis on offense is to get runners on base and hope to drive them in with a 3-run homer.

ankles to eyebrows. Expression yelled at an umpire to imply that his strike zone is from the batter's ankles to his eyebrows.

answer the call. Term used when a player is able to play or pitch when it is necessary for him to do so.

any given day. Refers to the belief that 'on any given day' a bad team can beat a good team.

any way on. Expression yelled at a batter to encourage him to get on base any way he can.

Appalachian League. An advanced rookie league within minor league baseball.

apple. Slang term for a baseball.

A

Appy League. Short for Appalachian League.

arbitration. When a third party is used to determine a settlement during negotiations between a player and an organization regarding the player's financial compensation in relation to his performance.

area guy. A name for a professional scout who is usually assigned at least five states to cover for his major league organization.

arm-side run. Term for a pitch that breaks towards the same side of the plate as the pitcher's throwing arm.

arm speed. Refers to the velocity of a pitcher's arm movement while throwing a ball.

around the horn. Phrase describing the action of throwing the ball from third base to second base to first base or vice versa, usually after an out is made.

arsenal. Term meaning 1) the assortment of pitches a hurler can use in a game, or 2) the offensive hitting weapons a team has at its disposal.

artificial surface. Astroturf or other synthetic grass surface.

assist. Term for when a player throws the ball to a teammate and his teammate records an out.

atom ball. Term for a ball hit right at a defender.

atta boy. Expression used as encouragement; short for that a boy.

attack the ball. To hit aggressively.

at the helm. Refers to coaching or managing a baseball team.

at the wheel. Refers to coaching or managing a baseball team.

automatic out. Refers to a player who is a poor hitter.

avg. A. Abbreviation for batting average against; a player's batting average against a particular pitcher (hits divided by at bats).

avg. Abbreviation for batting average (hits divided by at bats).

ax. Slang term for a baseball bat.

Quiz Picture #1

Babe Ruth is dead. Expression yelled at a pitcher to encourage him to throw strikes because Babe Ruth is dead and no other hitter is as great as Ruth.

bacalao. Spanish term used to describe a horrible or brutal baseball player.

back at the wheel. Refers to a person who is coaching or managing again.

backdoor curveball. A pitch that initially appears to be outside but curves and catches a part of the outside corner of the plate.

backs against the wall. Term for when a team that is playing in a game that they must win to stay in contention for a division or league championship.

back side. The opposite field.

backstop. Slang for a catcher.

back-to-back flags. To win a championship two years in a row.

back-to-back jacks. Refers to two home runs hit in succession.

back-up slider. A pitch that has the spin of a slider but stays on the inside corner of the plate.

back up the box. Term for when a ball is hit right back at the pitcher.

backwards K. Term meaning to strike out looking at the pitch instead of swinging.

backyard brawl. An intense rivalry between two teams that are located close to each other.

bad blood. Refers to two teams that have an intense rivalry.

bad hop. When a batted ball takes an unusual bounce as an infielder approaches to field it.

bad team chemistry. When teammates don't get along on or off the field; this usually hinders the players from playing up to their potential.

bad wing. Refers to a player who has an injured throwing arm.

bag. Slang term for a base.

baggy. Name for a pullover shirt that many players wear for batting practice.

bag of ones. Slang for the number eleven.

B

bail out. Term for 1) when a pitch makes a batter duck, flinch, or fall back because he thinks he is about to be hit, or 2) when a relief pitcher enters a game with inherited base runners and proceeds to get his team out of that jam without allowing any runs to score.

baiting. When an umpire purposely induces a coach or manager into an argument so as to cause an altercation and subsequent ejection.

balance point. Refers to the point in a pitcher's mechanics when he momentarily lifts his leg and balances before moving his body toward home plate.

balk. When a pitcher makes an illegal move while maintaining contact with the pitcher's rubber; as a result, all base runners move up one base.

balk move. A great pickoff move to first base by lefthanders, often a move that actually is a balk.

ball club. A baseball team.

balled it. Term used by umpires that means to call a pitch a ball.

baller. Refers to a person who plays the game very hard.

ballgame. Term for when the last out is recorded and a game is over.

ball is covered. Term for when a ball is hit very hard.

ball player. A person who plays baseball.

ball yard. A baseball field or facility.

Baltimore chop. An expression used to describe when a ball is hit hard off of home plate or the hard dirt around the plate causing the ball to bounce straight up.

banana turn. Slang expression for the turn that a base runner makes, between home and first, when he recognizes that the ball is safely into the outfield.

band box. Refers to a ballpark where a lot of home runs are hit; usually a park where the outfield fence dimensions are short.

bandwagoner. A fan who only supports a team when they are winning.

bang-bang play. Term for a very close play at a base.

banger. Term for a very close play.

bar arm. Refers to a batter straightening his front arm when he swings; this makes his swing long and slow.

bare down. To concentrate and get mentally focused.

barnburner. Refers to a very exciting baseball game.

barrage. Term used when a lot of players on a team hit the ball very hard.

barrel above the hands. Instructional phrase yelled at a batter so he will keep the bat up, giving him a better chance of hitting a line drive and less probability of popping the ball up.

B

baseball ballet. A graceful play in the field.

baseball junkie. An avid baseball fan.

baseball people. Term for many scouts, front office administrators, managers and general managers who are experts on baseball.

baseball purist. A fan who likes things "the way they used to be."

base clogger. Refers to a slow-footed player who hinders other base runners from normal advancement.

base hit…ball four. Phrase yelled at a batter as encouragement to get on base by a hit or a walk.

base hit him. Phrase yelled at a batter as encouragement to get a hit.

base knock. Slang term for a base hit.

base rap. Slang term for a base hit.

bases chucked. Slang term meaning the bases are loaded.

bases drunk. Slang term meaning the bases are loaded.

bases juiced. Slang term meaning the bases are loaded.

bases swept clean. Phrase used when a batter drives in all of the base runners with a hit.

bash brothers. Name for the combination of Mark McGwire and Jose Canseco, teammates in the late 1980's for the Oakland Athletics.

bashed. Term for a ball that is hit very hard.

basher. Name for a player who consistently hits the ball very hard.

basket catch. A waist-high catch made with the palm of the glove facing up.

batter, batter, what's the matter. A youth league chant to bother the opposing team's batter.

batter's box. The designated area in which a batter stands during an at bat.

batter up. Term that the umpire yells to begin an at bat.

battery. Term for a team's pitcher and catcher during a game.

battle. Word used to 1) encourage players to compete hard, or 2) describe a hard fought contest.

Bay Area Series. Refers to the 1989 World Series between the Oakland A's and the San Francisco Giants; a half an hour before Game Three an earthquake measuring 7.1 on the Richter scale hit the bay area forcing the series to be postponed for ten days.

BB. Abbreviation for base on balls.

BBWAA. The Baseball Writers' Association of America.

be a lead off. Phrase yelled at a batter to encourage him to be a good leadoff hitter; get on base; see a lot of pitches.

bean ball. A pitch that hits a batter.

B

bean ball war. Expression describing a game in which a number of hitters have been thrown at and hit by the opposing pitchers; when pitchers begin to throw at the opponent's batters in retaliation for their team's batters getting thrown at and hit.

beat the odds. Refers to a team or player who accomplishes something that was very unlikely to have occurred.

be a wall. Encouragement for the catcher to be a good blocker.

before it's all said and done. Expression used in reference to a player's or team's future.

beisbol. Spanish word for baseball.

belted. Term for ball that is hit hard.

bench-clearing rumble. A fight between players from opposing teams.

bench jockey. A reserve player who runs his mouth from the bench.

bench warmer. A reserve player who plays very little.

bender. Slang term for a curveball.

bend yer back. The classic youth league cliché shouted by uninformed coaches and parents to try to get a pitcher to get the ball down.

Bermuda triangle. Expression for the area in a ball park where a ball can be hit and three converging fielders can't catch it.

berry. Short for strawberry; a skinned area, usually around the knee, that typically results from sliding.

be patient. Term used to remind a batter to wait for a pitch that he can drive.

be selective. Term used to remind a batter to only swing at pitches he can handle.

be the man. Encouragement for a player to give a good performance, play well.

BF/9. Abbreviation for batters faced per nine innings.

BF. Abbreviation for batters faced.

big ball. Term for a strategy where the major emphasis on offense is to get runners on base and hope to drive them in with a homer.

big bats. Refers to a team's power hitters.

big boys. Term for the third, fourth, and fifth batters in a lineup.

big club. The major league team within a professional organization.

big dogs. Term for a team's top power hitters and run producers.

big downer. Slang term for a great downward-breaking curveball.

big fly. A home run.

big guns. Term for a team's top power hitters and run producers.

big hammer. Slang term for an outstanding breaking ball.

B

big league call up. When a player gets called up to a big league team.

big leagues. Major league baseball.

big market team. A major league team located in a big television market, which increases the amount of revenue that can be generated through broadcasts; this helps to determine payroll available for the ball clubs.

big mo. Slang term for momentum.

Big Red Machine. Refers to the Cincinnati Reds of 1975 and 1976.

bigs. The big leagues - major league baseball.

big shooter. Expression used as 1) a nickname for a player who acts like a big shot; or 2) a term of endearment for a teammate.

big timer. A player who acts like a big shot or has a 'better than you' attitude.

Billy Buck. Distracting phrase yelled at a first baseman when he is attempting to field a soft ground ball near the bag; in reference to Bill Buckner's crucial error in Game Six of the 1986 World Series.

bird dog. Name for a very low ranking professional scout; usually a non-paid volunteer.

bite. Expression used when a batted ball is in the air and the offensive team hopes it hits the ground before a fielder can catch it.

BK. Abbreviation for balk.

Black Sox scandal. Reference to a scandal involving eight members of the 1919 Chicago White Sox who were accused of fixing games for money; all eight were eventually banned from baseball for life.

blanked. When a team gets shut out.

blanks. Term for when a pitcher does not give up any runs.

blast. A ball that is hit very hard.

bleeder. A softly hit ball.

Bless You Boys. Refers to the slogan for the 1984 World Champion Detroit Tigers.

blistered. Term for when a ball is hit very hard.

blister the ball. To hit the ball very hard.

block. Term for what catchers do to keep pitches in the dirt from getting by them.

block and scramble. A drill for catchers where they block a ball and then quickly get to their feet, find the ball, and scoop it into their mitt.

blockbuster trade. A trade that usually involves several great players.

blooper. Term for 1) a softly hit fly ball, or 2) a series of funny plays featured on a highlight show.

blow a gasket. Expression meaning to lose one's temper.

blow it wide open. Phrase describing when a team scores so many runs that winning the game is out of reach for the opposing team.

blow out the lip. A grounds keeping technique using a high pressure water hose to eliminate a high area in the grass at the edge of the dirt where dirt and sand have built up.

blow up. Term for when a pitcher loses his temper and becomes less productive.

blue. Popular term for an umpire, referring to his uniform color.

blue darter. Slang term for a hard hit line drive.

bluff. When a base runner fakes a jump as if he is going to attempt to steal a base.

blunder. A mistake.

boards. Term for the outfield fence.

bobble. To juggle the ball.

bomb. A home run.

bombarded. Expression used when a pitcher gets hit very hard.

bonus baby. An old term describing a highly drafted player who gets a lot of money up front just to sign a contract.

book inning. The fifth inning of a nine-inning game; a pitcher must complete five innings to be eligible for a win.

book pitch. A widely used strategy to get batters out by throwing fastballs inside and breaking pitches away.

book strike. The strike zone according to the baseball rulebook.

boot. Slang term for an error.

boo ya. An expression used to celebrate a great hit or play.

borderline pitch. A pitch thrown close to the strike zone.

both ways blue. Expression yelled at an umpire to remind him to treat both teams the same.

bottom fell out. An expression used 1) when a split-finger fastball or forkball sinks at home plate, or 2) when things start to go bad for a team after they were initially going well.

bottom half. Refers to the second half of an inning when the home team bats.

bounced. When a player or coach gets ejected from a game.

bounced around. Phrase describing a player who has played for a lot of different teams and organizations.

bounced out. When a batter hits a ground ball and is put out.

bow yer neck. Expression yelled as an encouragement for a teammate to bare down and get tough.

box man. An old name for a pitcher.

box score. A listing of statistics for a baseball game.

boys of summer. Phrase referring to all baseball players.

BP: Abbreviation for batting practice.

BP top. The style of shirt players wear during batting practice.

brawl. A fight between players from opposing teams.

break 'em off a little something something. Phrase yelled at a pitcher to encourage him to throw a great breaking ball.

breaking ball. A curveball or slider.

break it up. Expression that refers to the hindering of a middle infielder from turning a double play by sliding hard into second base.

break out. Term of encouragement yelled to a batter to end a hitting slump.

break the mitt. A technique used by catchers to prepare to catch a pitch.

break the tape. Term for when a base runner approaches first base and he leans his upper body forward to appear to get to the base before his foot actually touches the base, much like track runners do at the end of a race.

breather. An easy game.

brew crew. Popular name for the Milwaukee Brewers.

brick hands. Term for a poor-fielding player who has a lot of balls bounce off his glove.

bringing it. When a pitcher is throwing the baseball very hard.

bring it on. Phrase yelled to try to intimidate the opposing team.

bring the nasty. Expression yelled as encouragement to the pitcher to throw the ball hard.

bring the noise. Term meaning to throw the ball hard.

bring the pain. Expression yelled as encouragement to the pitcher to throw the ball hard.

broke in. Refers to when a player first became a major leaguer.

broken bat single. When a player gets a base hit even though he breaks his bat.

Bronx Bombers. The New York Yankees.

Bronx cheer. Term for 1) sarcastic cheering after a bad umpire gets a call right or 2) when a team that has given up a lot of runs finally gets someone out.

brouhaha. Slang term for a fight during a baseball game.

brush-back pitch. A pitch thrown on the inside part of the plate, often near the batter's head.

bucket, giant, whip. Name of a technique to teach children how to throw properly; reach down in a bucket behind you to pick up the ball, slap the giant behind you in the chin, and crack the whip as you throw toward your target.

buckle me. Phrase yelled at an opposing batter when a breaking ball causes his knees to buckle under him.

buena linea. A Spanish term for hitting a good line drive.

Bugs Bunny change. Name of a certain grip used to throw a change-up.

bulge. The size of the lead a team has in the standings.

bulldog. Term for a player who is hard-nosed, very aggressive, and self confident.

bullet. An extremely hard hit ball.

bullpen. The area in a ballpark where the pitchers warm up on a practice mound.

bullpen by committee. When a manager uses his relief pitchers interchangeably.

bully. A nickname for the bullpen.

bump. Slang term for the pitcher's mound.

bunt. A softly tapped ball which is suppose to go a short distance on the infield; no swing of the bat is involved.

bunt for a base hit. A drag bunt executed in an attempt to get a hit.

bunt strikes. Phrase yelled at a batter when he is called upon to execute a sacrifice bunt.

bureau guys. Term for professional scouts employed by the Major League Baseball Scouting Bureau; they scout players and make reports that all major league teams use on draft day.

bury the head. Term meaning to hit a baseball with the barrel of the bat.

Busch. Refers to Busch Stadium, home of the St. Louis Cardinals.

bush. Term for a team or player acting in an unprofessional or unsportsmanlike manner.

busher. Name for a player who acts unprofessional in his actions or with his mouth.

bush league. Term for a team or player acting in an unprofessional or unsportsmanlike manner.

business end of the bat. The thick part of the bat where players hit the ball.

businessman's special. A mid-week day game in a city that usually plays their games at night; these frequently take place on a getaway day.

bust out the whippin' stick. Phrase that means to beat a team badly.

bust up two. Expression yelled at a base runner to encourage him to go in hard at second base in hopes of disrupting an infielder from turning a double play.

butcher. A terrible defensive player.

butcher boy. Term for a play where the batter fakes a bunt and then pulls the bat back to swing.

B

buy a ticket for the gun show. Sarcastic expression used for a player who egotistically pulls his shirt sleeves up so his biceps will show.

buy a ticket next time. Phrase usually yelled at a pitcher who didn't cover or back up a base after the ball was in play.

buyers. Term for contending teams that trade for players near the July 31 trade deadline.

by ya. Expression yelled at an opposing batter after he strikes out.

Quiz Picture #2

Quiz Picture #3

CABA. Continental Amateur Baseball Association; for players ages nine to adult.

Cactus League. Major league baseball's spring training league in Arizona.

California League. An Advanced A league within minor league baseball.

called up. Term for when a player is promoted to the next level in professional baseball.

call to arms. Term for when a team looks to their pitching staff in hopes that someone will give them a strong performance.

call to the pen. When a pitcher is brought into the game from the bullpen.

call up. When a team promotes a player to the next level in professional baseball.

came on like gangbusters. Phrase describing a team that plays very hard and makes a strong charge or improvement in the standings.

came roaring back. When a team that was losing rallied to make a game close.

came through in the clutch. Phrase used to describe a player who delivered a great performance in a tough situation.

campaign. Term for a baseball season.

camped under it. Expression for when a fielder is standing and waiting to catch a fly ball.

candlesticks. When one run is put on the scoreboard in consecutive innings.

candy. Short for candy hop.

candy hop. Term for an ideal bounce to a fielder who throws the runner out.

cannon. Term for a strong throwing arm.

can of corn. An easy fly ball.

cans. A conditioning technique using soda cans filled with sand or rocks to strengthen the small muscles of the shoulder that make up the rotator cuff.

C

can't break a pane of glass. Phrase used to imply that a pitcher throws very slow.

can't find the handle. When a fielder is trying to grab the ball but can't get a grip on it.

can't hit his weight. Term used to imply that a player's batting average is lower than his weight.

can't miss. A label put on a prospect who is almost certain to be a future major league star.

can't solve him. Expression describing a team that is shut down by a pitcher or pitchers on any given day.

canvas. Another name for a tarp, or tarpaulin that is put on the infield when it rains to keep the field from getting wet.

capitalized. Took advantage of a situation.

captain. A player who is designated as a dependable representative for the baseball team.

captain hook. Term for 1) a manager who is quick to yank a pitcher from a game, or 2) a great curveball.

cardinal sin. Phrase used when the fundamental codes of baseball, i.e., don't make the first or third out at third base and don't bunt or steal with a big lead are not followed.

career year. The best year in a player's career.

Carolina League. An Advanced A league within minor league baseball.

carpet. Term for Astroturf and other synthetic playing surfaces.

carry at the top. Term for a fly ball that carries well.

carrying their water. Phrase meaning that another team beats a team that your team is competing with for a championship.

castle. Term for the area around a catcher where every ball that bounces should be blocked.

cast off. A player who is let go by a team that no longer wants him.

catalyst. A player who gets on base in front of a team's power hitters.

cat and mouse game. Expression used when strategy is employed in some aspect of a baseball game.

catbird's seat. Phrase meaning to be in first place in your division.

catch and throw guy. A good defensive catcher who receives and throws well.

catcher's box. Designated area where a catcher begins each play during a baseball game.

catcher's gear. Catcher's equipment.

caught looking. Term for when a batter takes a third strike without swinging.

caught napping. Expression for when a player is put out because he was not concentrating on the job at hand.

caught the backdoor. Term for a pitch that is thrown over the outside corner of the plate.

cellar dweller. A last place team.

center the ball. To hit a ball almost perfectly in the middle.

CERA. Abbreviation for earned run average when catching.

cerebral. A term for an intellectual, deep-thinking player who brings an analytical approach to the game.

CG. Abbreviation for complete games.

CGL. Abbreviation for complete game losses.

CH. Abbreviation for chances (number of balls hit to a particular player).

chalk's free at Elwood's. An old Saline County, Illinois saying for when a squibber or cue-ball shot is hit spinning up the line; Elwood's was a local pool hall.

change of pace. Term for a change-up pitch.

change speeds. When a pitcher throws pitches at a variety of speeds to keep the batter off balance.

charge one outta here. To hit the ball out of the park.

charges. Term for the players on a baseball team.

charley horse. A cramp or stiffness in a player's muscle(s).

chased. Term meaning 1) to knock a pitcher out of a game in the early innings, or 2) to get ejected from a baseball game.

chatter. Expression describing the noise made when players talk, yell, or chant during a game.

chaw. A large amount of chewing tobacco in a player's jaw.

cheapie. A weakly hit ball that falls in for a hit.

cheap seats. Ballpark seats that are a long way from home plate.

cheat. Term for 1) when a player or coach breaks the rules in an attempt to win a game, or 2) a baserunning strategy where a player on third base runs on the batter's contact with the ball.

check. A word yelled at the home plate umpire to appeal a check swing.

cheese. Slang term for a hard pitched ball.

chew. Chewing tobacco.

chicken wing. Term for when a batter's front elbow is away from his rib cage area.

chicks dig the long ball. A saying made famous in a television commercial by Greg Maddox and Tom Glavine.

chink. A softly hit ball.

chin music. Term for a pitched ball near the batter's head.

C

chirp. When a team runs their mouth or talks trash.

choke and poke. Phrase meaning to choke up on the bat to protect the plate.

choker. A player who does not perform under pressure.

choke up. To move one's grip toward the barrel of the bat.

chopped. Term for when a ball is hit hard into the ground and takes several hops before a fielder can reach it.

chopper. A batted ball that takes several bounces, with one bounce usually going very high in the air.

chuck and duck. Term for when a pitcher throws a weak pitch and then has to duck to avoid getting hit in the head when the ball is hit back at him.

chunk. Slang term meaning to throw a baseball.

circle the wagons. When a fielder turns in several directions or in a circle while trying to catch a fly ball.

circus. Term for a defensive play that makes a joke of the game by combining a series of errors.

circus catch. A great catch, usually by an outfielder diving for the ball; a crazy looking play when a fielder has to battle the elements to catch the ball.

clash. A match up between two teams.

cleaned their clock. Phrase meaning to beat a team badly.

clean the bases. When a batter drives in all of the base runners with a hit.

clean up. Term for the fourth batter in the lineup.

clean up hitter. The fourth batter in the lineup.

clicker. Term for 1) a piece of equipment that umpires use to remember the count, and 2) a piece of equipment used to keep track of the number of pitches a pitcher has thrown.

climb the ladder. Phrase meaning 1) to get a batter to swing at a pitch that is up in the strike zone, or 2) when a pitcher throws strikes after a 3-0 count.

closed mouth. Term for a type of communication between the shortstop and second baseman to determine who will cover second base on a steal attempt; a closed mouth means "you have the bag" while the other fielder responds with an opened mouth which means "I have the bag."

close the door. When a relief pitcher comes into the game and keeps the other team from winning.

clout. Expression for a ball hit very hard.

club. Term for 1) a baseball bat, or 2) a baseball team.

clubby. Name for a person who is a clubhouse manager.

clubhouse. The home dressing room for a baseball team.

clunker. A softly hit ball.

clutch. Term for a player who excels under pressure.

clutch performer. A person who plays well in pressure situations.

cock. A movement batters make to prepare their upper body to swing.

coil. A movement batters make to prepare their upper body to swing.

collapse. When things fall apart for a team.

collar. A batter is said to wear this if he has no hits in a game.

come-backer. A ball that is hit right back to the pitcher.

come out of your shoes. Phrase yelled at a batter when he swings the bat very hard.

comes from the land down under. Phrase meaning 1) a pitch thrown sidearm by a submarine-type pitcher, or 2) a player from Australia.

come up big. Expression meaning to play great in a key situation.

commander-in-chief. Name for the head coach or manager.

concede the run. When a team's infielders play back at normal depth with a runner at third base and are willing to trade a run for an out or possible double play.

confab on the mound. Term for several players meeting on the pitcher's mound.

conference. When a coach goes to the mound to talk to his pitcher.

contact period. The period of time when coaches are allowed to make off-campus recruiting contacts and assess a player's talent.

contender. Term for a team that has a legitimate chance to win their division or league.

contraction. The theory held by some major league baseball administrators that the league needs to reduce the number of major league franchises for economic reasons.

control their own destiny. Term for a team that doesn't have to count on another team to help them win a championship.

cookie cutters. Refers to ballparks built during the 1960's which all looked very much alike, doubled as a football stadiums, and often had Astroturf playing surfaces, i.e., Veterans Stadium, Busch Stadium, and Three River's Stadium.

corked bat. A wooden bat that has a hole drilled into it and cork put in the hole, whereby the cork makes the ball travel farther when hit.

corks one. Term meaning to hit a long fly ball.

couldn't hit water if he fell out of a boat. Phrase used to imply that a player is a terrible hitter.

count. The number of balls and strikes charged to a batter during one at bat.

country swinger. A pitcher who is a fairly good hitter.

courtesy move. Term for a soft throw to first base by a pitcher with a base runner on first.

cracker jack. A good young baseball player with loads of potential.

crack player. A good young baseball player with loads of potential.

crane dip. Term for a large amount of dip tobacco in a player's mouth.

crank. Expression meaning to hit the ball hard.

creamed. Term describing 1) a ball hit very hard or 2) a team beaten badly.

cream puff. An easy team to beat.

cream rises to the top. A phrase describing the theory that great players will eventually play great in important situations.

creep. When a defensive player takes short choppy steps to generate momentum as the pitcher delivers the ball.

crew. Term for 1) a baseball team, or 2) a group of umpires working a game.

crew chief. The head umpire of an umpiring crew.

critical mass. An expression meaning time in a game when the outcome is decided.

crooked numbers. Numbers larger than one put up on the scoreboard.

crop. Term for a recruiting class.

cross checker. A high-ranking scout who usually watches a prospect play after an area scout has highly recommended the player.

crossed him up. When a pitcher threw a pitch other than what the catcher was expecting.

crossed up. When a pitcher and catcher each think a different pitch is to be thrown.

crow hop. A small hop that fielders take just before they throw to help generate momentum.

crown. Term for a championship of some type.

crunch time. Expression used to describe the time in a game when the tension is high, the game is on the line, and the outcome is decided.

crush. To hit a ball exceptionally hard.

crushed ice. Term for a home run.

crush job. A ball hit exceptionally hard.

CS. Abbreviation for caught stealing.

cuadrangular. A Spanish term for a home run.

cue ball shot. A ball that is hit off the end of the bat and spins.

cuff. Short for the rotator cuff; a group of four muscles in the shoulder that are often injured by pitchers.

cunny thumper. Slang term for a soft throwing pitcher; usually a left-hander.

cupcake. An easy team to beat.

cup of coffee. Term for a player who is called up to the big leagues for a short period of time.

curse of the Bambino. Refers to an alleged curse on the Boston Red Sox that keeps them from winning the World Series due to the fact that they sold Babe Ruth to the New York Yankees early in his career.

cursory move. When a pitcher makes a soft throw to first base with a runner on.

curtain call. When a player comes out of the dugout following a great accomplishment on the field to acknowledge the crowd's cheers.

cushion. Term for the distance between a team and their closest competitors.

cuspidor curvers. An old name for spitball pitchers.

customers. Baseball fans.

cut down. To be thrown out while baserunning.

cut 'er loose. Term meaning to swing a bat or throw a ball very hard.

cut off man. An infielder who positions himself about half way between the outfielder throwing the ball and the base he is throwing to; the infielder cuts off the throw if the ball is off line or will not make it to the target in time to get the base runner out.

cut off the run. When infielders play even with their bag or move up onto the infield grass looking for a play at home plate.

cutter. A pitch that moves at the last instant, like a slider.

cutting the grass. Term for when a player, during a squeeze play, cuts through the infield grass from second base to home; this only works with a two man umpiring crew.

CWS. Abbreviation for the College World Series.

cycle. A batter who hits a home run, triple, double, and single in one game.

D-1. NCAA Division One; the largest schools and best collegiate teams play in this division.

D-2. NCAA Division Two; schools that are typically smaller than the Division One schools play at this level.

D-3. NCAA Division Three; this non-scholarship level of college baseball includes smaller schools, many of which are very academically oriented.

dance floor. Term for the infield.

date with destiny. Term for a player who is on the verge of doing something great, i.e., pitching a no hitter, breaking a record.

dead air. Expression for a ballpark where a ball hit to the outfield does not carry very well.

dead ball era. Refers to a time in the early 1900's when very few home runs were hit and the game was played in a one-base-at-a-time style.

dead fish. A change-up pitch.

dead heat. When two or more teams trying to finish in first place have similar records.

dead period. The time when coaches are not allowed to make in-person recruiting contacts or assessments; they cannot make on-campus or off-campus, official or unofficial visits to see potential players.

dead red. Term for when a batter is primarily looking for a fastball.

dead to rights. Expression used when a player is thrown out by a large margin.

dead weight. Term for a player who keeps a team from reaching their potential.

deal. A trade between two teams.

dealer. Slang term for a pitcher.

dealing. Pitching.

deals. When a pitcher throws a pitch.

debacle. Description of sloppy or terrible play.

decision. When a pitcher of record gets a win or a loss.

decoy. To fake or fool the opposition.

deek. Short for decoy; to fake or fool the opposition.

delay. Term for a delayed steal, when the runner at first base takes two aggressive shuffle steps and then accelerates towards a base as the pitch is crossing home plate.

delivers. When a player comes through with a good performance in a pressure situation.

delivery. The motion of throwing a pitch.

deluge. Term for 1) when a team gets a lot of runs in a hurry, or 2) a rain downpour while playing a baseball game.

dem bums. An affectionate nickname for the Brooklyn Dodgers used by their loyal fans.

demoted. When a player is sent to a lower level of professional baseball.

dented the plate. Expression meaning to score a run.

deposit. Term for when a home run is hit into the seats.

deuce. Term for 1) a curveball or 2) a name for number two.

deuces. Term for a two balls, two strikes, two out count, or when players hold their hats upside down and shake them side to side for good luck on this count.

deuces wild. A count of two balls, two strikes, and two outs.

DH. Abbreviation for designated hitter or doubleheader.

dial 8 for long distance. Phrase used when a player hits a home run.

D

diamond. A baseball field.

diamond in the rough. Term for a player who has natural ability but is not yet a good player.

did he go? Question asked by a home plate umpire to a base umpire to help determine whether the batter swung or checked his swing.

didn't come to play. Phrase describing a player or a team that appears to not be mentally focused or is not playing hard.

dime. A nickname for number ten.

dimer. A nickname for number ten.

dime slider. Term for a tight-spinning slider that shows a circle the size of a dime to the batter.

ding-dong. Slang term for a home run.

ding-dong the pitch is dead. Phrase used by some announcers when a batter hits a deep home run.

dinger. Slang term for a home run.

director. A head coach or manager.

dirty. Term for a nasty pitch.

dish. Slang for home plate.

disposed of. When a team gets a batter out.

DL. Abbreviation for the disabled list.

do a catch. Throw a baseball back and forth, play catch.

do a job. Phrase yelled at players to encourage them to make fundamental plays.

doctor the baseball. When a pitcher purposely cuts or disfigures a baseball or puts any illegal substance, i.e., spit or Vaseline, on the ball to give himself an unfair advantage.

doctor the bat. When a batter illegally alters a bat, i.e., with cork or pine tar.

dog. Term for 1) a lazy baseball player, 2) an underdog.

dog days. Term for the very hot days of July and August; it is hard to play through the fatigue caused by the extreme heat.

dogfight. A hard-fought contest.

dog pile. When players run out on the field to celebrate and pile onto each other.

dogging it. When a player loafs or is being lazy on a play.

do it large. Term meaning to hit the ball a long way.

do or die. When a player must make a play.

don a uniform. To put on a team's uniform.

dong. Slang for a home run.

donnybrook. A fight between players on two opposing teams.

don't be too fine. Phrase yelled at a pitcher to encourage him to throw strikes and stop nibbling around the plate.

don't fall in love with the sugar. Phrase used to remind a pitcher not to throw his off speed pitches too often.

don't go there. Phrase yelled after a home run is hit.

don't kill it just meet it. A country saying yelled to a batter to remind him to not swing too hard while trying to get a hit.

don't let him in. Term yelled to encourage a batter to not strike out.

don't let the ball play you. Encouragement yelled to a fielder to be aggressive and not sit back on a ground ball and give the ball a chance to take a bad hop.

don't overthrow. Advice yelled at a pitcher who is trying to throw too hard at the expense of changing his proper mechanics.

don't shut the barn door if the horse is already out. Expression meaning to not throw the ball to the base behind the base runner.

don't take the bat out of his hands. Phrase yelled at a base runner to remind him to not do something stupid that will prevent a good run-producing batter from getting a chance to bat with runners on base.

door knocking knuckles. Term for the knuckles that should be lined up when gripping a bat.

doormat. A last place team.

double cut. Term for when a hit goes to the wall and both the shortstop and second baseman go out into the outfield to be the cutoff men.

double dip. Term for 1) a double-header, and 2) a double play.

doubled off. When a base runner is caught in a double play.

doubleheader. When the same two teams play two games back-to-back on the same day.

double switch. A lineup change in which a new pitcher and fielder come into the game and the pitcher assumes the position in the batting order farthest away from the current hitter.

douse out the flames. When a relief pitcher enters a game and stops a rally.

dove headlong. Term for a player who left his feet and dove head first to try and catch a ball.

down and dirty. Phrase yelled as encouragement to play the game hard.

down bite. Term for a breaking ball that has a sharp downward action.

downhill. Phrase yelled at a pitcher to remind him to follow through.

down in order. When the defense retires the first three batters of an at bat.

down on strikes. To strike out.

down on the farm. The minor leagues.

down stairs. A low pitch that is out of the strike zone.

down the home stretch. Term for the last part of a baseball season.

down the slope. Phrase yelled at a pitcher to remind him to follow through.

dozen. Nickname for number twelve.

DP. Abbreviation for double plays.

draft and control. Refers to a drafted high school player who goes to a junior college for a year of evaluation by professional scouts; the organization owns the rights to sign the player for one year.

draft and follow. Refers to a drafted high school player who goes to a junior college for a year of evaluation by professional scouts; the organization owns the rights to sign the player for one year.

draft coverage. Refers to major league area scouts who have the primary responsibility for scouting high school and college baseball players for the amateur draft.

drag. Short for drag bunt, a bunt attempted for a base hit.

drew first blood. Term used to describe the team that scores first.

D

dribbler. A weakly hit ground ball that goes through the infield for a hit.

drill. Term meaning 1) to hit a batter with a pitch, or 2) to hit the ball very hard.

drill shot. To hit the ball very hard.

driver's seat. Phrase used to describe a team that 1) is currently in first place, or 2) is in a great position to finish first or win a game.

dropped off the table. Expression used to describe an outstanding curveball.

droppy. An Australian term for a curveball.

drop some zeros. Encouragement for a pitcher to pitch shutout baseball over a number of innings.

duck snort. Slang for a softly hit fly ball that drops in for a hit.

ducks on the pond. Term used when the bases are loaded.

duel. A very competitive ballgame.

dummy sign. Signals given by a coach that are not live and no play is on.

dump. Term for a very bad baseball facility.

dumped. To be ejected from a game.

dump payroll. Refers to teams that are out of the pennant race near the July 31st trade deadline. They often trade high-priced players who are in the last year of their contract, to contending teams for the stretch drive.

dump salary. When a team tries to trade a high-priced player, usually near the July 31st trade deadline in order to reduce their payroll.

dunker. A softly hit fly ball that falls in for a hit.

dying quail. A softly hit fly ball.

dynasty. Term for a team that has won a number of championships and has a great tradition for winning.

Quiz Picture #4

E. 1) Abbreviation for an error, or 2) term yelled at an opponent when he makes an error.

E1. Abbreviation for an error on the pitcher.

E2. Abbreviation for an error on the catcher.

E3. Abbreviation for an error on the first baseman.

E4. Abbreviation for an error on the second baseman.

E5. Abbreviation for an error on the third baseman.

E6. Abbreviation for an error on the shortstop.

E7. Abbreviation for an error on the left fielder.

E8. Abbreviation for an error on the center fielder.

E9. Abbreviation for an error on the right fielder.

earnie. Slang for ERA, or earned run average.

earthquake series. Refers to the 1989 World Series between the Oakland A's and the San Francisco Giants; a half an hour before Game Three an earthquake measuring 7.1 on the Richter scale hit the bay area forcing the series to be postponed for ten days.

Eastern League. One of the AA leagues within minor league baseball.

east-to-west curveball. A curveball thrown by a right-handed pitcher that breaks right-to-left.

effectively wild. Term used to describe a pitcher who is just wild enough to keep hitters off balance and uncomfortable.

efus pitch. Slang for a lob pitch.

EH. Abbreviation for extra hitter; occasionally used in youth baseball instead of a designated hitter.

eight hole. The eighth batter in the line up.

El Birdos. The nickname of the 1967 World Series Champion St. Louis Cardinals as a result of many key players being of Hispanic descent.

el foldo. Slang term meaning to collapse, choke, or fold.

elements. The weather conditions.

emery ball. Term for when a baseball is illegally roughed up by an emery board or nail file in order to get the ball to sink in an unnatural way.

empty the bases. To get a hit that drives in all of the base runners.

ER. Abbreviation for earned runs.

ERA. Abbreviation for earned run average (number of earned runs divided by the number of innings pitched times nine = ERA).

evaluation period. The time when coaches are allowed to be involved in off-campus activities to appraise a potential recruit's academic credentials and athletic ability; an in-person, off-campus recruiting contact with a prospect is not authorized.

even the score. Term meaning 1) to get revenge on another player or team; or 2) to tie a game or series.

every fifth day. Refers to a starting pitcher's workload within a five-man rotation.

excuse me swing. Term for a weak swing; much like a check swing.

execution. The performing of a fundamental aspect of the game.

exhibition game. A game that does not count in the official standings.

exit stage left. Phrase used to describe a home run hit to left field.

exit stage right. Phrase used to describe a home run hit to right field.

expand the zone. When a catcher sets up on the extreme outside corner of the plate in order to get the batter to swing at a close pitch.

extend the inning. When a player gets on base with two outs and keeps an inning alive.

extinguish the blaze. When a relief pitcher enters a game and stops a rally.

extra frames. Slang for extra innings.

extra innings. When a game is tied after nine complete innings, the game goes into extra innings until a winner is determined.

extras. Short for extra innings.

extreme. Term for a pitch thrown six-to-twelve inches off the outside corner of the plate.

eye black. The black substance applied under the players' eyes to help reduce glare from the sun.

40-man roster. The number of players who are "on the club" going into spring training; being on this roster does not mean they will start the regular season with the big club.

40-40 man. A player who hits 40 home runs and steals 40 bases in the same season.

faced the minimum. Phrase used when a pitcher has faced the fewest number of batters possible in an inning.

face the music. Expression used when a player enters a tough situation and is expected to come through in the clutch.

fair pole. Same thing as the foul pole, but some call it this because if it hits the pole it is a fair ball.

fair-weather fan. A fan who supports a team only when they are winning.

faithful. Term for a team's most loyal fans.

fake jump. When a base runner acts like he is going to attempt to steal a base.

fake stuff. Slang term for Astroturf or other synthetic surfaces.

Fall classic. The World Series.

fan. Short for fanatic, a loyal enthusiast of a team or the game of baseball.

fanned. Struck out.

fantasy camp. A camp with a spring training atmosphere where people spend time playing with retired major league baseball players.

farmhand. Term for a minor league player.

fat pitch. A slow pitch that is easy to hit.

FB. Abbreviation for fly balls and fly balls allowed.

feed. Term for when a player throws the ball to a fellow infielder in an attempt to get a force out or start a double play.

feel the noose. Phrase yelled at an opponent in the hopes that they will choke.

fielder's choice. An offensive statistic given to a hitter who reaches base on a play other than a hit or an error.

F

fighting tooth and nail. Expression that means to be competing vigorously.

filth. Slang term for a nasty pitch.

find a hole. To hit the ball where the fielders aren't positioned.

find a way. Encouragement yelled at teammates to come up with a way to win.

fireball. A pitch thrown very hard.

firebrand. Term for a feisty, hard nosed baseball player or coach.

fired. Term meaning 1) a hard thrown ball, or 2) to be removed from a job.

fired blanks. When a pitcher shuts out an opposing team.

fireman. Term for a relief pitcher, usually the team's closer.

firewood. A broken wooden bat.

first sacker. The first baseman.

fisted. To get jammed on a pitch close to the batter's hands.

fisticuffs. A fight between players on two opposing teams.

five eyes. Refers to a technique used to teach children to throw properly with their "five eyes" on their target; the "eyes" are the side front ankle, side front hip and side front shoulder along with their two real eyes pointed toward their target.

five hole. The fifth batter in the line up.

five man. Short for a five-man pitching rotation.

five o'clock hitter. A player who looks great in batting practice at five o'clock but can't hit well in a game at seven o'clock.

five tool player. Term for a prospect who is said to possess all five tools needed in professional baseball: 1) running speed, 2) arm strength, 3) ability to hit for power, 4) ability to hit for average, and 5) fielding ability.

flags. The pennants that are earned by winning a championship.

flair. A softly hit ball.

flair for the dramatic. Term used to describe a player who thrives on producing in pressure situations.

flake. Term for a player who is unusual.

flameout. Expression for a team that has recently lost a lot of games and is playing very poorly.

flame-thrower. A player who throws very hard.

flash. Term for the quick glance a batter may take to find the ball when he is a few strides out of the batter's box.

flashes the signs. When a coach gives signals to the players.

flash in the pan. A player who is very popular or successful for a short period of time and then fades from notoriety just as quickly as he appeared.

flash the leather. Term that means to play good defense.

flash the signs. Description for when a coach is giving signals to players.

FLD%. Abbreviation for fielding percentage (putouts added to assists and then divided by the total number of putouts, assists and errors equals fielding percentage).

fleet footed. Term for a player who can run very fast.

flip. Term for 1) a softly tossed ball, or 2) a game played in a circle where players try to control the baseball by flipping it with their gloves while trying to make the other players miss.

flip a coin blue. Derogatory remark yelled at an umpire implying that his judgment is so bad it would be better if his decisions came from a flip of a coin.

flip downs. The traditional style of sunglasses for baseball players that are flipped down only when they are needed.

flip it over. To turn a double play.

flip one over. To turn a double play.

flip two. To turn a double play.

floater. A very slow pitch that seems to float to the plate.

floating zone. Term for a very inconsistent strike zone called by an umpire.

Florida State League. An Advanced A league within minor league baseball.

fluke. Term that can refer to an inferior team winning a game.

fly. To run very fast.

F

fly out. When a batter hits a fly ball that is caught for an out.

fold. Term used for a team that plays well for a period of time and then begins to lose consistently.

force the issue. Term for when a team plays aggressive baseball in the hopes that the other team will make mistakes.

foreign substance. Any illegal substance, such as spit or Vaseline, that is put on the ball to give a pitcher an unfair advantage.

forfeit. When the chief umpire declares a team the winner without finishing a game.

forkball. A split-finger fastball that is slower than a fastball and usually drops right at the plate.

forty man. Refers to the forty-man roster that includes the players officially "on" the ball club going into spring training.

foul pole. The poles along the right and left field foul lines that help determine whether a ball is fair or foul.

foul tip. A ball that barely hits the bat during a swing and then flies toward the catcher.

F

four-bagger. A home run.

four hole. The fourth batter in the line up.

four man. Short for four-man pitching rotation.

four-man crew. A team of four men who umpire a game; this type of crew is used in major league baseball.

four seamer. A pitcher's grip where they hold their index and middle fingers across two seams of a baseball so as it rotates, all four seams will move toward the plate.

FPCT. Abbreviation for fielding percentage.

FPS. Abbreviation for first pitch strike.

fracas. Slang for a fight between players on two opposing teams.

frame. Term for 1) an inning, 2) a receiving technique used by a catcher when catching a pitch, or 3) a player's build and body type.

franchise. A major league baseball organization.

franchise player. The most important and usually the best player in a franchise.

free agency. When a player is able to negotiate a contract with any team he chooses, usually signing with the highest bidder.

free agent. A player who is free to negotiate a contract with any team he chooses.

free baseball. Term for a game that goes extra innings.

free fall. When a team drastically drops in the standings due to a very long losing streak.

free for all. Term for a fight between players on two opposing teams.

free pass. A base on balls.

freeze on a liner. Advise yelled to a runner so he won't get doubled off.

Freshman campaign. Term for a player's first or rookie year.

friendly confines. Refers to Wrigley field, home of the Chicago Cubs.

front-foot hitter. A batter who has a hitting problem due to his lunging at pitches.

front-line arm. Term for a pitcher who possesses an arm that could enable him to someday become a big league ace.

front office. Where the team staff and executives work.

front-runner. A player who is great when his team is ahead but chokes when his team is losing.

frozen rope. Expression describing an exceptionally hard hit ball.

full count. When the count on a batter is three balls and two strikes.

full monty. Slang for the bases are loaded.

fun at the ole ballpark. Expression describing the joys of the great game of baseball.

fungo bat. A long, slim bat used to hit practice balls to fielders.

fungo circle. An area where coaches stand while hitting fungoes.

fungoes. Name for practice balls hit to fielders.

funky cheese. Slang for a pitch that has a lot of movement and is hard to hit.

funnel. A receiving technique a catcher uses where he catches the ball and moves his mitt towards his chest protector.

Quiz Picture #5

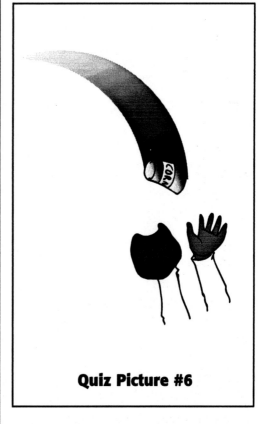

Quiz Picture #6

G. Abbreviation for games pitched or games played.

G.M. Abbreviation for a general manager.

gag. Term meaning to fold under pressure; to choke.

gain ground. A term used to describe 1) how a catcher blocks pitches by slightly moving outward and toward the plate at an angle, and 2) the act of moving out with momentum when receiving a pitch to be thrown on a stolen base attempt.

game face. A stern, concentrating look on the face of a player.

game is on the line. A time in a game when the outcome is to be decided.

game of inches. Expression used to describe baseball because so many plays are determined by inches.

gamer. Name for a player who steps up and plays his best in key situations.

games back. The number of games a team trails the first place team.

gamesmanship. A strategy that involves trying to get the psychological edge on an opponent.

gap. Left-center and right-center field.

garbage. A word 1) used to describe a very bad baseball player, 2) yelled at an opposing player when he commits an unsportsmanlike act, or 3) yelled at an umpire after a very bad call.

gas. A pitch thrown very hard.

Gashouse Gang. Refers to a colorful and jocular group of players for the St. Louis Cardinals in the 1930's.

gas it up. Slang term for throwing a ball hard.

gassed out. When a player is fatigued.

gave him an earful. When a player or coach gives an umpire a piece of their mind.

gave him a shave. Phrase used for a pitch that is high and tight; also referred to as chin music.

gavel. Slang for a baseball bat.

GB. Abbreviation for ground balls allowed.

GDP. Abbreviation for grounded into a double play.

gear. Baseball equipment.

gem. A great pitching performance.

get ahead change. A first pitch change-up thrown for a strike.

get ahead curveball. A first pitch curveball thrown for a strike.

get ahead fastball. A first pitch fastball thrown for a strike.

get a tin can and a monkey. Phrase yelled at people who constantly yell at the umpires and beg for calls to go their way.

get a W. To win a baseball game.

getaway day. The last day of a series in which the visiting team will leave town after the game.

get behind the ball. A fielding technique taught to outfielders whereby they get one step behind the location where they will catch the ball and then step up during the catch, creating momentum for the throw.

get dirty...we got soap. Phrase yelled at a player who should have slid but didn't.

get 'em next time. Encouragement for a team to win the next game they play.

get 'em on, get 'em over, get 'em in. Refers to the classic way to manufacture a run.

get him a bucket...he's throwing up. Derogatory comment yelled at a pitcher who continuously throws pitches up in the strike zone.

get in the game. Phrase yelled at a player to encourage him to concentrate or try harder.

get into the act. When a player joins his team in performing a particular feat.

get off me ball. Term for when a player hits the ball very hard.

get on your belly. Encouragement for a teammate to dive for the ball.

get on your horse. Phrase describing a player who must run as hard as he can to catch a fly ball.

get outta town. Term yelled during a home run.

get out the broom. Phrase used, often by fans, after sweeping a series.

gets down the line. Term used to describe a hitter with outstanding speed.

gets it through the zone. A batter who possesses outstanding bat speed.

get that weak stuff outta here. Expression yelled at a pitcher to tell him that his pitches are weak.

get the ball down. Instruction yelled to a pitcher telling them to throw pitches lower in the strike zone.

get the kids off the swing. A derogatory statement yelled at a poor hitter.

get the rabbit on. Encouragement to the leadoff man, who usually possesses good speed, to get on base.

get up baby. Term yelled when a long fly ball is in the air and may not be high enough to get over the outfield fence.

get your elbow up. An instructional phrase used to help a batter improve his swing.

get your tailgate down. An instructional phrase to remind a fielder to get his glove on the ground.

get your tools on. A phrase used to tell a catcher to put his equipment on.

getting shelled. When a pitcher is getting hit very hard.

gettin' splinters. Term for a player who plays very little and sits on the bench a lot.

GF. Abbreviation for games finished.

giant killers. Term for a traditionally weaker team that has a knack for upsetting favored teams.

giddiup on the ball. Description of a pitch thrown with great velocity.

give 'em a piece of your mind. When a player or coach tells an umpire what they think of their umpiring.

give 'em a run for their money. To compete hard and give another team a good game.

gives chase. Term for when a fielder runs after a fly ball to try to catch it.

give the ball a ride. Phrase yelled as encouragement for a batter to hit the ball a long way.

give yourself up. To lay down a bunt or hit behind a base runner to help the team manufacture a run.

glove to the heart. Term describing the proper place for the pitcher's glove (glove side chest) while he is throwing the ball.

go ahead man. The player who scores the run that gives a team the lead.

go ahead run. The run scored that gives a team the lead.

goat horns. What a player is said to wear if he caused his team to lose, i.e., be the goat.

go-getter. An aggressive player who constantly works hard.

go hard or go home. Term used to encourage players to play the game with maximum effort or not play at all.

go in hard. To slide hard into a base in hopes of disrupting a defensive player.

going deep. Hitting a home run.

going down to the wire. Refers to a tight pennant race that might not be decided until the last days of the season.

going downtown. Hitting a home run.

going to the downs. Phrase meaning to run around the bases quickly.

go out and get him. To go to the mound and pull a pitcher from a game.

go quietly. Term for when a team goes three up and three down in an inning.

go right after him. Phrase yelled at a pitcher to encourage him to just throw strikes and not try to hit the corners.

go right at him. Phrase yelled at a pitcher to encourage him to just throw strikes and not try to hit the corners.

go to your room. Derogatory phrase yelled at an opposing batter after he strikes out.

go with the pitch. When a batter hits an outside pitch to the opposite field.

go yard. Hit a home run.

golden sombrero. Term for when a batter strikes out four times in one game.

gold glover. A big league player who is voted the best defensive player in the league at his position.

gone fishing. Slang for a swing at a pitch that was in the dirt.

good action. Term for a pitch that has a lot of movement.

good baseball man. Term for many scouts, front office administrators, managers and general managers who are experts of the game of baseball.

goodbye Mr. Spalding. Refers to an old saying yelled when a home run was hit.

good eye. Term for a batter who has a good command of the strike zone.

good man behind you. Phrase yelled at a batter as encouragement that the next batter is a good hitter.

good nucleus. A good core group of players on a team.

good ole' country hardball. Refers to a good fastball.

good one coming. Encouragement yelled at a batter that he is about to see a good pitch to hit.

good team chemistry. When teammates get along well together; this is usually instrumental in a team's success.

good wood. Term meaning 1) to hit the ball hard on the sweet spot, or 2) a bat made with high quality wood.

goose eggs. Zeroes on the scoreboard.

gopher ball. Slang for a home run that a player has to "go for".

gorilla ball. A college term for a team that hits a lot of home runs as a result of using metal bats.

G

G

gork. Slang term for a weak base hit.

got a beat on it. When a fielder runs down a fly ball and catches it.

got all of it. Phrase used to describe a ball hit as hard as a player can possibly hit it.

got burned. Term for when a fielder misplays a fly ball and lets it go over his head.

got cut. When a player is let go from a team or organization.

got 'em baffled. Refers to a team that is shut down by a pitcher or pitchers on any given day.

got him looking. When a pitcher throws a third strike past a batter without him swinging.

got him to chase. When a pitcher gets a batter to swing at a bad pitch.

got his bell rung. Term for when a player gets hit very hard.

got hosed. Received a bad call by an umpire.

got lit up. When a pitcher's pitches get hit very hard.

got pegged. Term for when a base runner gets thrown out.

got robbed. When a batter gets a probable hit taken away from him because the opposition makes a great play.

got some pop. Term for a batter who possesses a powerful swing.

got the big head. Term for a player who is overly confident, which often ends up adversely affecting his performance.

got the hook. Derogatory phrase for when a pitcher is taken out of a game.

got their number. When a team seems to dominate another team for a long period of time.

got their signals crossed. A miscommunication during a baseball game.

got their wires crossed. A miscommunication during a baseball game.

go-to guy. Term for a team's best clutch performer; usually refers to a pitcher.

gotta come to him. When a pitcher must throw strikes to a batter because he can't afford to walk him.

gotta come to play. When a player or team must be mentally focused and ready to play hard.

gotta have ya. Phrase yelled at teammates to encourage them to play well.

grab some pine. Derogatory phrase yelled when an opponent strikes out.

grand larceny. Term for when a bad call is made against a team.

grand old game. A legendary nickname for baseball.

grand salami. Slang for a grand slam.

grand slam. A home run hit with the bases loaded, thereby scoring four runs.

grandstand. The seats behind home plate and down the baselines.

granny. Term meaning a grand slam.

Grapefruit League. Major league baseball's spring training league throughout the state of Florida.

graveyard. Term for a very large outfield that keeps more fly balls in the park and makes it harder to hit home runs.

gravity ball. Slang for a pitch so slow that it seems as if gravity pulls it down before it gets to the plate.

great AB. When a player works the count and sees a lot of pitches in an at bat.

great American pastime. Traditional nickname for baseball.

great at bat. When a player works the count and sees a lot of pitches.

great command. Term for when a pitcher possesses great control and consistently throws all of his pitches for strikes.

green light. When a player has the manager's approval to swing at a pitch or steal a base on his own.

green monster. Refers to the left field fence at Boston's Fenway Park.

grip it and rip it. Country saying that refers to picking up a bat and swinging it hard.

grooved. Term describing a pitch thrown right down the middle.

ground out. When a batter hits a ground ball and is put out.

ground rule double. Refers to a batted ball that bounces off the ground and goes over the fence, automatically awarding the batter a double.

GS. Abbreviation for games started.

GSH. Abbreviation for grand slam home run.

guard the plate. Encouragement yelled at a batter with two strikes on him to not strike out.

gun. Slang term for a strong arm.

gunfight. Slang for a great pitchers' duel.

guns. Word meaning 1) a player's biceps, 2) pipes.

gun shy. Term describing a player who is scared of the ball after being hit.

gunslinger. Name for a tough pitcher.

Gwynn drill. Refers to a hitting drill named after legendary hitter Tony Gwynn; during batting practice a batter hits the ball straight across from them in the batting cage; this is one of the best drills to teach batters to 1) see the ball deep into the strike zone, 2) keep their hands inside the ball, 3) keep their front elbow down and slightly touching the rib cage, and 4) hit the ball efficiently to the opposite field.

H

H. Abbreviation for hits and hits allowed.

hack. Slang for a hard swing.

hacker. A player who swings the bat wildly and very hard.

half way. When a base runner goes halfway between two bases on a fly ball.

hammer. Term for a great curve ball.

handcuffs. A youth league term for a fielding technique on ground balls in which the inside part of both wrists remain touching. This contributes to a quicker release and provides a safety factor since a bounding ball will hit the palm of the fielder's hand instead of his face.

handful. Term for a tough opponent.

hands inside the ball. A hitting technique using a short, quick swing that enables a batter to hit to all fields.

hang 'em up. To quit playing baseball.

hanger on'er. A veteran player who keeps hanging on in hopes of getting promoted.

hanging slide piece. Slang for a hanging slider.

hang out a rope. To hit the ball hard and on a straight line.

happy zone. Term meaning right down the middle of the strike zone, where a hitter can drive the ball.

hard hands. Expression for a fielder who appears to have a hard glove that does not give with the ball and locks the fielder's elbow.

hard luck loser. Term for a pitcher who pitches a good game but still gets the loss.

hard nosed. A phrase describing a tough, gritty player who plays the game all out.

Harvey's Wallbangers. Nickname of the 1982 American League Champion Milwaukee Brewers.

has been. A player whose best playing days are behind him, usually because of age.

hat trick. Slang term for when a player strikes out three times in a game.

have a catch. To throw a baseball back and forth; play catch.

have a day. Expression of congratulations said to a player who is having a great day on the field.

have the corners covered. Slang for having base runners on first and third.

HBP. Abbreviation for hit by pitch.

headache. Term yelled to alert someone to watch out for a flying ball.

head case. A player who is emotionally unstable or who has attitude problems.

head check. Term for when a hitter quickly turns his head to see where the ball is while he is still only about four strides out of the batter's box. If it is into the outfield he should make a turn at first, if it is being played by an infielder he should sprint through the first base bag, break down, and look to his right in case there is an overthrow.

head high. The proper target while playing catch and where to aim when throwing a ball during a game.

headhunter. Name for a pitcher who has a reputation for throwing at batter's heads.

heading down the homestretch. The last part of baseball's regular season.

heading North. Term used by players after they break spring training camp.

heads. Warning yelled to alert people to watch out for a flying ball.

he can flat fly. An expression that means a player can run very fast.

he can float. An expression that means a player can run very fast.

he can go. An expression that means a player can run very fast.

he can pick 'em up and put 'em down. An expression that means a player can run very fast.

he can scoot. An expression that means a player can run very fast.

he can't hit the broad side of a barn. Phrase describing a poor hitter.

he hits 'em in bunches. Term for a player who hits a lot of home runs in a short time.

he'll take the ball. Term for a pitcher whose arm is consistently ready to pitch.

he's got a Howitzer. Expression describing a player with a strong throwing arm.

he's lookin' for a walk. Phrase yelled to imply that the batter does not want to hit; that he is only at the plate to draw a walk.

hearing footsteps. Phrase used to describe the pressure on a first place team when contenders are close to catching them.

H

heart and soul. Term for the emotional leader and stabilizing force on a baseball team.

heart of the order. The number three, four and five batters in the batting order.

heart of the plate. Right down the middle of the plate.

heat. Slang for a ball thrown very hard.

heavy ball. A mysterious phenomenon that happens while playing catch; some player's throws seem to hurt the hand more and the ball feels heavier when caught.

heavy hitter. A hitter who possesses good power.

heavy lumber. Term for a big baseball bat.

helmsman. A manager or head coach.

helps his own cause. When a pitcher does something productive on offense to help him get a victory.

here comes that man. Expression used when a particular player who performs well against a particular team comes to the plate; this saying is the origin of the nickname for Stan "The Man" Musial; fans in Brooklyn would say "here comes than man again" because during his career he hit very well against the Dodgers.

hey-batter-batter-batter. A youth league chant yelled at a batter to annoy him.

high A. The highest of three levels of Class A minor league baseball.

high and tight. Term for a pitch thrown on the inside part of the plate, usually near the batter's head.

high heat. A fastball up in the zone.

high strike. A pitch at the top of the zone that is called a strike.

high water mark. Refers to the point in a season when a team has its maximum number of victories over the .500 mark.

highway robbery. When a team is the victim of a horrible call by an umpire.

hill. Slang for the pitcher's mound.

hill leader. Term for a team's ace pitcher.

hill spots. Refers to each pitcher's spot in the rotation.

hind catcher. A southern name for a catcher.

hit a pill. Term meaning to hit a hard line drive.

hit a seed. Term meaning to hit the ball very hard.

hit-and-run. An offensive play in which the base runner(s) take off running and the batter is responsible for hitting the ball on the ground to the right side to avoid the base runner(s) getting thrown out.

hit 'em where they ain't. An old saying encouraging a batter to hit the ball where the fielders are not playing.

hit for the cycle. To hit a single, double, triple, and home run in one game.

hit it a country mile. When a batter hits the ball a very long way.

hit like a missile. Term for a ball hit very hard.

hit on the button. Term for a ball hit very hard.

hit on the nose. Term for a ball hit very hard.

hit on the screws. Term for a ball hit very hard.

hits a run. A reminder yelled at a batter that a hit would drive in a run.

hits to all fields. Term describing a player who has the ability to hit the ball to all parts of the ballpark.

hit the ball where it's pitched. Expression meaning that a batter should pull an inside pitch, hit a ball down the middle to center, and hit an outside pitch to the opposite field.

hit the bricks. Slang for when the fans leave a ballgame.

hit the bull. Phrase yelled at a wild pitcher; refers to a famous line from the movie "Bull Durham."

hit the cut. Phrase yelled at an outfielder to remind him to hit the cutoff man.

Hit the Road Jack. A song sung by fans at many ballparks when an opposing pitcher or position player is taken out of a game.

hit the showers. Derogatory phrase yelled at a player when he is removed from a game.

hit the skids. To be in the middle of a very bad slump or losing streak.

hit the top of the ball. Instruction given to a batter so he won't pop the ball up; advice to help a batter hit a line drive.

hit the weight room. Derogatory phrase yelled at an opposing batter who hits a fly ball that is caught at the warning track.

hitter's count. When a hitter has the pitch count in his favor.

hitter's eye. Refers to the dark colored section just above the center field fence that helps batters see the ball better when it is pitched.

hitter's park. Term for a ballpark that has smaller dimensions and is more conducive to hitters hitting home runs.

hitting bb's. Slang term for when a player hits a lot of balls very hard.

hitting pellets. Slang term for when a player hits a lot of balls very hard.

hit your spots. Instruction yelled at a pitcher to encourage him to have good control and hit the catcher's target.

H

H

hold. A statistical category for relief pitchers that shows how many base runners they inherited when they entered the game actually scored.

hold him on. When an infielder, usually a first baseman, stands next to a base that has a base runner on it to help keep the base runner's lead to a minimum due to the threat of the pitcher throwing to the base.

holding. Term for someone who has chewing tobacco or dip.

hold your ground. Instruction yelled to 1) an infielder telling him to keep his defensive position even if a hit-and-run or straight steal is employed, or 2) a batter so he will stay tall and not bail out on a curveball.

hole. Slang for a dugout.

hole in his swing. Term referring to the place in the strike zone where a batter is vulnerable.

holy cow. Exclamation said after a great play; made famous by hall-of-fame announcer Harry Caray.

home cookin'. Term for when a home team gets all of the close calls from the umpiring crew because of home team favoritism.

home field advantage. The advantage a team might have due to playing at home in front of their own fans.

homer. Term for 1) a home run, or 2) an umpire who shows favoritism toward one team.

homered. Term that means 1) to get cheated because of the way an umpire calls a game, or 2) when a player hits a home run.

home stand. A consecutive number of games played at home.

hook. Slang for a curveball.

hop. Term for 1) the velocity on a pitch, or 2) the way the ball bounces.

hope springs eternal. Refers to an optimistic outlook during the preseason because every team still has a chance to win a pennant.

horsehide. Slang for a baseball.

horse race. Term referring to a close finish to a tight pennant race.

horseshoe. The part of a baseball's seams that looks like a horseshoe; used as a grip on certain pitches.

hose. Slang for a strong throwing arm.

hosed. Term meaning 1) to receive a bad call, or 2) to be thrown out.

hot as a firecracker. Expression describing a player who is in the midst of a hot streak.

hotbox. Term for when a base runner is caught between two bases and is trying to avoid being tagged out.

hot corner. Common term for third base.

hot dog. A show-off.

hot stove. Refers to discussions in the winter about the upcoming baseball season.

house that Ruth built. Refers to Yankee Stadium, home of the New York Yankees.

how about that. Expression used after a great play; made famous by hall-of-fame announcer Mel Allen.

HP/PA. Abbreviation for hit pitches per at bat.

HR. Abbreviation for home runs and home runs allowed.

hula hoe. A piece of equipment that is used to dig up grass in a straight line at the edge of the grass portion of a baseball field; pronounced "HOO lee ho" in the South.

hum baby. Phrase yelled to encourage a pitcher to throw the ball hard.

hummer. A ball that is thrown hard.

hump. Term for the pitcher's mound.

hump back liner. Slang term for a short fly ball.

hum that tater. Phrase yelled to encourage a pitcher to throw the ball hard.

hung out to dry. When a player gets stuck in a difficult situation, usually as a result of a teammate's failure to do what they were suppose to do.

hunnow. Slang for 'come on now'.

hurler. Another name for a pitcher.

hurries it up there. Term for when a pitcher throws hard.

H

Quiz Picture #7

I

IBB. Abbreviation for intentional base on balls.

If a cow can't eat it…I don't want to play on it. Statement made by a player who was against Astroturf and in favor of baseball fields made of grass.

If it ain't broke…don't fix it. An old adage meaning that if a player is successful playing a certain way, don't try to change him.

If you build it they will come. A famous line from the baseball movie "Field of Dreams".

igniter. A player who gets on base in front of a team's power hitters.

I must be in the front row. Refers to a famous saying by Bob Uecker as he sits in his "Uecker seats" at the top of the stadium.

in a funk. Term for a player who is going through a bad streak.

in a jam. Crucial situation in a game when the other team is about to score.

in a pinch. A difficult situation in a baseball game.

in a tailspin. Term describing a team that is playing very poorly and has recently lost a lot of games.

in-between hop. A bouncing ball that does not give a fielder a normal hop to allow him to field it easily.

in-coming. A warning shouted out when a ball is about to land in an area where people are located.

in contention. When a team has a legitimate chance to win their league or division.

indicator. What a coach touches, while flashing signs, to let his players know which live sign is on.

inherited base runners. The base runners already on base when a relief pitcher enters a game.

in his tracks. When a player stops instantly.

injury bug. Term for when a team gets hit with a number of injuries in a short period of time.

inked. Term for when a player has signed a national letter of intent, or a professional contract.

INN. Abbreviation for innings.

inning eater. A pitcher who has the stamina to throw a lot of innings.

I see 'ya workin'. Phrase yelled at a batter as he works the pitcher deep into the count.

I-70 series. Refers to the 1985 World Series between the St. Louis Cardinals vs. the Kansas City Royals; Interstate 70 connects the two cities.

inside move. A type of pick off move to second base.

inside-the-park home run. When a batter hits a home run without the ball going over the outfield fence.

Instruct. Abbreviation for instructional league baseball.

intangibles. Skills and performances by players that help their team become successful but don't show up in the statistics or box score.

intentional pass. An intentional walk.

intentional walk. When a pitcher deliberately walks a batter.

International League. AAA league of minor league baseball.

in the groove. When everything seems to be going right for a player.

in the hole. Two batters away from being up to bat.

in the hunt. When a team is in contention for a division or league championship.

in the throes. Refers to being in the midst of some type of streak or trend in performance, i.e., a hitting streak,
winning streak, or hitting slump.

in the zone. When a player is at the top of his game.

into the humanity. Phrase used when a ball is hit into the stands.

in ya. To psychologically get into the opponent's head.

in your kitchen. An extreme inside pitch.

in your wheelhouse. An ideal pitch to hit, thrown right down the middle.

IP. Abbreviation for innings pitched.

IPS. Abbreviation for innings per start.

IRA. Abbreviation for inherited runs allowed.

Iron Mike. Refers to a one-armed pitching machine that holds hundreds of balls, which enables hitters to get numerous swing repetitions.

issued a pass. Walked a batter.

issued a walk. Walked a batter.

it ain't over 'til it's over. An old Yogi Berra cliché meaning that a team is never out of a game until the last out is recorded.

it ain't over 'til the fat lady sings. An old cliché meaning that a team is never out of a game until the last out is recorded.

it might be...it could be...it is...a home run. The famous home run call of hall-of-fame announcer Harry Caray.

it's gonna play. Term for when a player is able to catch a fly ball.

I

J

jack. A home run.

jacked. Term for 1) when baseball pant legs are pulled up to the knees, or 2) when a ball is hit very hard.

jack-of-all-trades. Term for a player who can play many different positions.

jake legging it. Expression meaning to loaf on a play.

jam. Term for 1) when a person hits the ball on the narrow part of the bat, or 2) a crucial situation in a game when the other team is threatening to score.

jam job. When a batter hits the ball on the narrow part of the bat.

jam sandwich. Slang for when a pitch jams a batter.

jelly legs. Slang for when a batter's legs buckle after a nasty curveball is pitched at him and then curves away.

jobbed. When a team loses a call or a game because an umpire shows favoritism.

Johnny Wholestaff. Refers to when a manager uses the whole staff in a game.

johnson. A home run.

journeyman. A veteran player who has played for a number of teams.

JUCO. Abbreviation for a junior college.

juggle the lineup. When a manager or head coach changes the usual batting order to try and get more productivity from his offense.

juiced. Term for 1) a hard hit ball, or 2) balls that are wound tighter than usual, causing an unusually high number of home runs.

juiced ball. Term for one of a batch of balls from the factory that seem to "jump off the bat", causing an increase in the number of home runs.

jump on the ball. Phrase meaning 1) to get a good first reaction to a hit ball, or 2) good velocity on a ball.

jump on the bandwagon. Term for a person who only supports a team when they are winning.

June swoon. A losing steak in major league baseball that happens in the month of June.

Junior circuit. The American League.

Junior loop. The American League.

junk. Slang for slow breaking pitches or pitches out of the strike zone.

junkballer. A pitcher who throws without much velocity and usually throws a lot of breaking balls.

junk dealer. Slang for a pitcher who throws without much velocity and usually throws a lot of breaking balls.

just make contact. Encouragement yelled at a batter to remind him to put the ball in play.

just off the plate. A pitch that is close to the corner of the plate but barely misses being a strike.

just takes one. Phrase yelled at a batter as a reminder that no matter what the count is, it only takes one pitch to get a hit.

just throw strikes. Encouragement for a pitcher to throw strikes.

just what the doctor ordered. Term used when something happened that was exactly what a team needed at that particular juncture of the game; often said after the team has turned a double play.

Quiz Picture #8

J

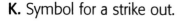

K. Symbol for a strike out.

kangaroo court. Where teammates facetious take each other to "court" for things such as not hustling, acting like a big timer, or just about any other reason; players found guilty by the "jury" are fined, with the proceeds usually going towards a post-season party.

keep pace. When a team wins a game and stays the same number of games behind a team ahead of them in the standings.

keep the knob down. Phrase yelled at a batter as encouragement to not pop the ball up.

keep your eye on the ball. Instructional phrase used to help a batter concentrate on watching the ball when hitting.

keystone. Slang for second base.

Khorey League switch. An old saying from Saline County, IL used when the pitcher and catcher switch positions in the middle of an inning.

kick. Term for 1) an error, or 2) when an umpire makes a bad call he is said to kick a call.

kick it around the lot. To make a fielding error.

kick yer dog blue. A derogatory phrase yelled at umpires inferring that they are blind and need a seeing-eye dog.

killer instinct. Term for when a player has the ability to finish off an opponent and not let them off the hook.

kill the ball. Term for 1) when catchers block pitches, or 2) when a ball is hit hard.

kiss it goodbye. Phrase used after a player hits a home run.

knee buckler. A pitch that causes a batter's knees to buckle under him.

knock. A home run.

knockdown pitch. A pitch that is high and tight, meant to send a message to the other team; sometimes thrown in retaliation for one of the pitcher's teammates getting knocked down.

knock it down. Instruction yelled at an infielder to make sure he keeps the ball in the infield.

knockout blow. A play that seals a victory for a team.

knuckle dragger. Term describing a pitcher who lets his glove drag on the ground while he throws the ball; this puts undue stress on the throwing shoulder and could lead to him injuring his shoulder.

KO'ed him. Slang for knocking a pitcher out of a game.

K

Quiz Picture #9

Quiz Picture #10

L. Abbreviation for a loss.

laced. Term for when a ball is hit hard.

lack of run support. When a team scores very few runs for a pitcher.

laser. A hard hit or hard thrown ball.

laser beam. A hard hit or hard thrown ball.

laser show. Derogatory term yelled at the opposing pitcher when he is getting shelled.

late bloomer. A player who develops his skills later than most players.

late life. Term describing a pitch that moves or breaks right at home plate.

late push. When a team makes a move late in a season to compete for a championship.

late surge. When a team makes a move late in a season to compete for a championship.

latter part of the lineup. The seventh, eighth, and ninth batters in the lineup.

laughingstock. Term for a team that is so bad that others laugh at them.

launch a salvo. When a player hits a ball very hard.

launched. When a ball is hit very far.

launching pad. A ballpark where a lot of home runs are hit.

lay him down. Instructions to a pitcher to throw a knockdown pitch at a batter.

lay off that junk. Phrase yelled at a batter to remind him not to swing at pitches out of the strike zone.

lay one down. To bunt the ball.

lay out. To dive for a ball.

lead. Short for leadoff.

leather man. Slang for an excellent fielder.

leave. To hit a home run.

leaving. Hitting a home run.

left the building. Term for when a home run goes over the fence.

left throw. A technique used when fielding a slow grounder; the ball is fielded with the left foot forward and knees bent, then the upper body raises up and the ball is thrown overhand with the right foot maintaining contact with the ground.

lefty. A left-handed player.

Legion ball. American Legion Baseball; for players of high school age.

let's play two. Famous adage by the legendary Ernie Banks of the Chicago Cubs.

level it out. Encouragement yelled at a batter to hit a line drive.

lid lifter. Refers to the first major league game of the season that traditionally use to be played in Cincinnati; recently the lid lifter has been played in different foreign countries.

light him up. Encouragement yelled to a batter to hit the ball very hard.

line drive. A hard hit ball with very little arc.

line drive in the book. Common term said to a player who gets on base as a result of a weak hit.

liner. A line drive.

lip. High area in the grass at the edge of the dirt where dirt and sand have built up; lips are a problem for infielders because they can cause bad hops.

little ball. Strategic emphasis on bunting, stealing, and the hit and run; trying to play for one run.

little bingo. Slang for a base hit.

Little League. The most famous youth baseball organization for players ages five to eighteen; the best teams in the world at the nine through twelve year old age group play in the legendary Little League World Series in Williamsport, Pennsylvania.

lit up. When a pitcher gets hit hard.

live arm. Term for a player with great arm strength.

loaded bat. A wooden bat that has had cork added to the core of the wood to make the ball travel farther.

load one up. To throw a spitball.

loaf. To be lazy.

LOB. Abbreviation for runners left on base.

lock and load. A term for a batter who swings as hard as he can on every pitch.

locked in. When a player is very focused and concentrated on the task at hand.

locking horns. Two teams involved in a hard fought game.

lofted. A ball that is hit very high.

lollipop curve. A very slow, easy-to-hit breaking ball.

lollygagger. A player who loafs on a play.

Lonborg and champagne. The headline that ran in a Boston newspaper the day of Game Seven of the 1967 World Series; it implied that the series was wrapped up for the Red Sox

L

because their ace, Jim Lonborg, would beat St. Louis Cardinals ace Bob Gibson; many experts believe this turned out to be another curse on the Red Sox (see Curse of the Bambino) as the Cardinals won the game 7-2; a famous scene in Cardinals history is the St. Louis players celebrating with champagne as they chant "Lonborg and champagne."

longball. A home run.

long barrel. A softly hit ball that slices to the opposite field.

long ride. A home run.

long strike. Term for a long foul ball.

long suit. A team or player's strengths.

look alive. Instruction yelled at players to get them to wake up and concentrate.

lookin' for a walk. Phrase yelled at an opposing batter that implies that he does not really want to hit, but is only at the plate to draw a walk.

loop. A baseball league.

loose. 1) when a player's arm is prepared to throw at full speed, or 2) when a player's legs are prepared to run at full speed.

losing streak. When a team loses a number of games in a row.

lost his bid. Usually said after a pitcher gives up a hit after he carries a no-hitter into the late innings of a game.

loud out. When a hard hit ball is caught for an out.

low A. The lowest of the three levels of Class A minor league baseball.

low riders. Term for the style of baseball pants that go down to the ankles.

L screen. The protective screen, shaped like an "L", that batting practice pitchers stand behind.

lugged into it. To swing very hard.

lumber. Slang for a wooden baseball bat.

lunge. When a batter commits his weight too early during a swing and becomes off balance.

Quiz Picture #11

Mackey Sasser syndrome. Term for a catcher who is psychologically hindered from making basic throws back to the pitcher.

magic number. The number that is a combination of team wins and opponent losses that allows a team to clinch a division championship.

major league pop-up. Term for a pop fly that is hit extremely high in the air.

make a charge. When a team makes a strong run at winning a game or a pennant.

make him chase. Instruction yelled at a pitcher to remind him to throw a pitch out of the strike zone in the hopes that the batter will swing at it.

make him come to you. Instruction yelled at a pitcher to remind him to throw strikes to a batter.

make him leave there running. Reminder yelled at a pitcher to not walk the batter.

make him stop. Phrase yelled at an umpire so he will make sure that a pitcher stops his hands or has a discernable change of direction while in the stretch.

make it be there. Encouragement yelled at a batter so he will only swing at strikes.

make it be yours. Encouragement for a batter to swing at a good pitch to hit.

make it reach. Encouragement yelled to fielders to remind them to make their throw reach their target on the fly, about head high.

makes quick work of. Term for when a pitcher easily and quickly retires a batter.

make sure he goes. Instruction yelled to a base runner before he starts to run on a three ball, two strike, two out count to make sure the pitcher throws towards the plate.

make the adjustment. Suggestion that a player change some part of his mechanics in order to improve.

make up call. When a team gets a favorable call by an umpire to make up for an earlier blown call that went against that team.

make up ground. When a competing team gets closer to the first place team in the standings.

make up. A description of a player that includes his maturity, psychological outlook, and competitive instincts.

mammoth blast. A very long home.

marker. A run.

marquee player. A star player who has a lot of fan appeal.

mash. To hit the ball very hard.

masterpiece. A superbly pitched game.

match up. A baseball game.

mauler. Term for a player who hits the ball very hard.

meat. Slang for a pitch lacking velocity and thrown right down the middle.

meat of the order. The third, fourth, and fifth batters in a batting order.

medi ball. A medicine ball; used by many baseball players to strengthen their abdominal muscles.

melee. A fight between players from two opposing teams.

Mendoza line. A .200 batting average; named after former big leaguer Mario Mendoza.

men in blue. Umpires.

mental block. What a player is said to have when he is psychologically hindered from making routine plays.

mental error. A mistake made by a player because of a lack of focus.

mental lapse. When a player makes a mistake as a result of a lack of focus.

merry-go-round. When the bases are loaded and the base runners take off on the pitch with a three ball, two strike, two out count.

mid A. The middle of three levels of Class A minor league baseball.

mid-major. A mid-size NCAA D-1 college or university.

Midwest League. A Mid A league within minor league baseball.

Miracle Mets. Refers to the 1969 World Champion New York Mets.

miscue. An error.

missile. A ball hit very hard.

mix it up. Term for 1) a pitcher who throws a number of pitches at varying speeds in order to keep the batter off balance, or 2) when players fight.

mix speeds. To throw pitches at various speeds in order to keep the batter off balance.

MLBPA. Major League Baseball Player's Association.

moment of truth. Term for the time in a game when the tension is high, the game is on the line, and the outcome is decided.

money ball. A home run.

money. Slang for a player who performs well under pressure.

monster shot. A long home run.

montro. Spanish term for a great baseball player.

moon shot. A high, towering home run.

mop up guy. A pitcher who comes in to throw when his team is getting beaten badly.

mound. The mounded area of dirt where the pitcher stands to pitch.

mound demeanor. The way a pitcher carries himself as a pitcher.

mound presence. How well a pitcher carries himself with confidence and competency while he is on the mound.

moves him off. Term for when a pitcher throws the ball high and tight.

move the baseball. Put the ball in play.

move the runner. When a batter either bunts or hits behind a base runner to move him into scoring position.

move up 90. To advance one base.

moving at a snail's pace. A game that takes a long time to play.

mowed 'em down. Term for when a pitcher impressively gets the other team out.

mr. snappy. A name for a curveball

that breaks sharply.

mudball. When a pitcher illegally applies mud to a ball to create an unfair advantage.

Mule Mix. Name of a type of drying agent that is put on dirt when it is wet.

murderer's row. Refers to the 1927 New York Yankees batting order.

muscled up. To hit with power.

mustard on the ball. Slang for a pitch that is thrown with great velocity.

must win situation. When a team is playing a game that they must win to stay in contention for a division or league championship.

MVP. Abbreviation for most valuable player.

M

Quiz Picture #12

nabbed. Slang for being thrown out.

NABF. National Amateur Baseball Federation; for players ages eleven to adult.

NAIA. National Association of Intercollegiate Athletics; typically small, private, religiously affiliated colleges compete in NAIA; the level of baseball talent generally ranges from mid-major Division 1 to poor Division 3.

nail in the coffin. Term for the play that seals a victory for a team.

nail it down. When a relief pitcher comes into a game and gets the save by ending the game.

nails. A tough, gritty, hard-nosed player.

nasty. Term for 1) a hard pitch to hit, or 2) a tough pitcher.

Nasty Boys. Refers to the 1990 World Series Champion's bullpen threesome of Randy Myers, Rob Dibble, and Norm Charlton.

national letter of intent. A document signed by a prospective student-athlete which states that he intends to enroll at a particular college.

national past it's time. Phrase used by some critics of baseball who believe that the games best days are in the past.

national pastime. A traditional nickname for baseball.

NBC. National Baseball Congress; a baseball league for men.

NCAA. National Collegiate Athletic Association; the governing body of the majority of college baseball.

NCCAA. National Christian College Athletic Association; association comprised of Christian colleges; typically regarded as the lowest level of college baseball; the best NCCAA teams usually also have a membership with the NCAA or the NAIA.

Negro Baseball League. The major league for non-white players before Jackie Robinson broke the color barrier in major league baseball in the 1950's.

neighborhood play. Term referring to the fact that many times during a double play a middle infielder is not required to actually touch the base as long as they are 'in the neighborhood'.

never make the 1st or 3rd out at third base. A self-explanatory cardinal rule of baseball.

newcomer. A first-year player.

New York-Penn League. A short-season A league within minor league baseball.

nibbler. Term for a pitcher who tries to throw his pitches on the corners and rarely throws a pitch over the middle of the plate.

nice kick Pele. Derogatory term used when an opponent's player makes an error.

nice spot. Encouragement given to a pitcher that he threw a good pitch.

nickel. A name for number five.

nightcap. The second game of a doubleheader.

nine hole. The ninth batter in the line up.

niner. A name for number nine.

NLCS. Abbreviation for the National League Championship Series.

NLDS. Abbreviation for the National League Division Series.

no brainers of hitting. Refers to the preliminary check points before a swing; these are fundamentals that a batter does not have to think about during a swing: 1) the back part of the shoe is parallel with the batter's box (toe slightly turned in) so as to maximize hip

power during a swing, 2) door knocking knuckles are lined up, 3) the top hand grip is golf-like, 4) the front elbow is slightly touching the rib cage, and 5) the front foot is lined up with the back foot (don't lock out hip rotation).

no cheat. A baserunning strategy for when there is a base runner on third; the base runner makes sure that the ball goes through the infield before running home.

no doubter. Term for a home run that was hit so hard that there was never a doubt it would go out of the park.

no looker. Term for a pitcher who, while having a runner on second, does not look at the runner before pitching the ball.

no love lost. When bad blood exists between two teams in an intense rivalry.

no man's land. Term for where a softly hit ball falls into the outfield and no fielder can get to it.

non-believer. A player who lacks self-confidence in his abilities.

no-no. Slang for a no hitter.

no place to put him. Expression used when the bases are loaded.

Northsiders. Refers to the Chicago Cubs.

north-to-south curveball. Term for a curveball that breaks downward.

Northwest League. A short-season A league within minor league baseball.

nosebleed section. Term for the seats at the top of a stadium.

nose dive. When a team is in the middle of a losing streak and losing ground in the standings.

not you. Term said to a batter after a strike call that his teammates thought was a ball.

now you're ready. Encouragement yelled at a batter after a questionable strike call.

NP. Abbreviation for number of pitches.

nubber. Slang for a ball hit very softly.

Quiz Picture #13

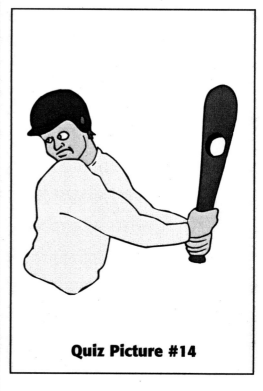

Quiz Picture #14

1 runner. A runner who possesses above-average speed.

123. Encouragement yelled at the defensive players to retire the first three opposing batters in order.

1B. Abbreviation for both a single and a first baseman.

o'fer. When a batter gets no hits in a game; to go "0" for.

Oakies. Abbreviation for Oakley; a popular brand of sunglasses used by baseball players.

OBP. Abbreviation for on base percentage (hits + walks + hit by pitch divided by at bats + walks + hit by pitch + sacrifice flies = on base percentage).

obstruction. When a fielder, who is not in the process of making a play or not in possession of the ball, hinders the advancement of a runner.

odds on favorite. A team that is strongly predicted to win their respective league or division.

OFA. Abbreviation for outfield assists.

off on the wrong foot. A bad begin-ning to a game or season for a player or a team.

off-speed delivery. Term for any pitch other than a fastball.

off the deck. Term for when a team ends a losing streak or a player ends a bad slump.

off the hook. When a pitcher of record leaves a game with his team losing, yet not end up being the losing pitcher because his team ties or takes the lead in the game.

off the schnide. Term for when a team ends a losing streak or a player ends a slump.

off to the races. Term for 1) a base runner stealing a base, or 2) a player who runs the bases fast.

OFP. Abbreviation for overall future potential; the major league base-ball scouting bureau evaluates a player's tools using a scale from 40-80.

oh doctor. An old phrase used after a great play.

old # 1. Slang for a fastball.

O

old # 2. Slang for a breaking ball.

old Abner has done it again. Term used to emphasize that a great game is in progress.

old school. Term for a traditionalist who deeply respects the traditions of baseball and loves the fundamental aspects of the game; loves to see the game played the 'right way'.

ole'. Derogatory term yelled when a fielder doesn't get in front of the ball; refers to a matador's move.

on a tear. A phrase used when a player is hitting the ball exceptionally well.

on deck. The batter scheduled to hit after the current batter.

one and done. Expression for a team that loses its first tournament game and is eliminated.

one bagger. Term for 1) a single, or 2) a first baseman.

one depth. When the infielders play at their normal defensive positions.

one hole. The first batter in the batting order.

one in the well. To get the first out.

one looker. Term for a pitcher who, while having a base runner on second, looks at the runner only once before pitching the ball.

one more biscuit. Expression yelled when a batter hits a ball to the warning track; implies that if he had eaten one more biscuit for breakfast he would have had enough power to hit the ball out of the park.

one of those days. A day when virtually everything goes right for one team and wrong for the other.

one pitch away. Phrase yelled when a team is one strike from a strike out or one ground ball away from turning a double play to end the inning.

one pitch…one spot. Encouragement yelled to a batter to be selective and swing at a pitch he can drive.

one tough cookie. A tough baseball player to play against.

one tough customer. A great baseball player; a player that is hard to beat.

one tough hombre. A tough baseball player to play against.

on fire. When a player is on a hot streak.

on his way to Cooperstown. Refers to a player destined to make it into the Major League Baseball Hall of Fame in Cooperstown.

on the docket. Term meaning that a game is scheduled.

on the hop. Encouragement yelled to remind a player to hustle.

on the hot seat. When a manager or coach's job is in jeopardy as a result of their team not playing up to expectations.

on the juice. A player who is taking steroids.

on the market. A player who is on the trading block.

on the mend. A player who has been injured but is getting better.

on the ropes. A pitcher on the verge of being knocked out of a game.

on the sack. To get on base.

on the shelf. A player that gets injured and can not play for a specific period of time; on the disabled list.

on the trading block. When a player is rumored to be included in trade talks.

on your belly. Encouragement yelled at fielders to dive for the ball.

on your toes. Reminder yelled to players to pay attention and be alert.

opened mouth. Refers to a type of communication between the shortstop and second baseman regarding who will cover second base on a steal attempt; opened mouth means "I have the bag" while the other fielder responds with a closed mouth which means "you have the bag".

opening day. The first official game of the season for a baseball team.

open the floodgates. When a team has a big rally going.

oppo. Short for opposite field.

optioned. When a major leaguer is sent to the minors.

out by a country mile. When a base runner is out by a long distance.

outed him. Term umpires use meaning to call someone out.

outfit. A baseball team.

out of contention. Term for a team that has little or no chance to win their division or league.

out of gas. When a player is tired.

out of options. After a player has played in the minor leagues for a certain amount of time, his major league team must keep him at the big league level and cannot send him back to AAA team.

out of their game. Term for a player who is trying to play beyond his capabilities or in a style that is different from what has been successful for him.

overtime. Extra innings.

over the boards. A home run.

over the shoulder catch. A catch made over the shoulder of a fielder, usually with his back to the infield.

overthrow. When a player throws a ball over his intended target.

o

P

PA. Abbreviation for plate appearances or the public address system.

Pacific Coast League. AAA league within minor league baseball.

pack it in. To give up.

paint the corner. Slang for a pitch that goes over the outer edge of home plate.

parked one. To hit a home run.

park it. To hit a home run.

passive lead. A non-aggressive baserunning lead in a sacrifice bunt situation.

past his prime. A player whose best playing days are behind him, usually because of age.

pasture. Slang for the outfield.

patsy. An easy team to beat.

pay off pitch. The pitch thrown when there are three balls and two strikes.

pay station. Home plate.

pay the price. To work extremely hard in physical conditioning and skill development in order to become the best possible player.

PB. Abbreviation for passed balls.

pea. A hard hit ball.

pearl. A new, white baseball.

peck of trouble. Term for when a ball is hit that will cause problems for the defensive team.

peg. Slang for a throw.

pennant drive. A team's effort to win a division championship.

pennant winner. The team that wins the championship in one of major league baseball's divisions.

pepper. A short game of throw and hit, generally played during warm-ups.

pepper pot. Term for a tough, gritty player.

perfect game. A game in which one team has no runs, hits, errors, or walks.

perfecto. Slang for a game in which one team has no runs, hits, errors, or walks.

perfect or foul. A drag bunting term meaning that the bunted ball should be very close to the line or foul; if the ball is bunted in the middle of the field the pitcher will almost always throw the batter out.

PFP. Short for pitcher fielding position; a drill where the pitcher practices covering first base with feeds from the first and second basemen.

physical specimen. A player who has an outstanding physique for baseball.

pick. Term for 1) when a team tries to pick off a base runner, or 2) fielding a ball after it has hit the ground.

pick it up. Encouragement yelled at players to get them to play harder.

pickle. Slang for when a base runner is caught between two bases and is trying to run safety to one of the bases.

pick me out a winner Bobby. A famous line from the baseball movie "The Natural."

pick one out. Encouragement yelled at a batter to swing at a pitch he can hit hard.

pick out a good one. Encouragement yelled at a batter to hit a good pitch.

pick play. When the defense puts on a play to try and pick off a base runner.

pick you one out. Encouragement

yelled at a batter to see a good pitch and hit it.

picture perfect. Term for when a fundamental of baseball is executed exceedingly well.

pilfer. To steal a base.

pilot. A manager or head coach.

pinch hitter. A substitute batter.

pinch runner. A substitute runner.

pine tar. Substance put on a bat to help hitters get a better grip on their bat.

pine tar game. Refers to a game in 1983 when George Brett of the Kansas City Royals hit a crucial home run in Yankee Stadium against the New York Yankees that was disallowed because he had pine tar too high up on his bat.

Pioneer League. An advanced rookie league within minor league baseball.

pipes. Slang for large arms.

pipes out. Slang for when a baseball player alters his uniform shirt so that more of his biceps show.

pitch around him. When a team avoids pitching to a dangerous hitter by intentionally walking him.

pitch count. The number of pitches a pitcher has thrown in a game.

pitcher of record. The two pitchers who, at any given time in a game, are responsible for either a win or a loss.

P

pitcher's best friend. Term for a double play.

pitcher's count. When a pitcher has the count in his favor.

pitcher's duel. Term for a game in which both pitchers are simultaneously pitching great games; typically a low scoring game.

pitchers employed. The number of pitchers a team uses in a single game.

pitcher's got a rubber arm. A derogatory youth league chant implying that the opposing pitcher has a weak-throwing arm.

pitcher's park. A ballpark with large dimensions, which is conducive to long fly balls being caught for outs.

pitching staff. All of the pitchers on a baseball team.

pitching triple crown. Term for when a pitcher leads his league in wins, earned run average, and strikeouts.

pitch out. When a pitcher intentionally throws the ball extremely far outside so the catcher can be unimpeded in trying to throw out a base runner attempting to steal a base.

PK. Abbreviation for pick-offs.

plastered. A ball that is hit very hard.

plated. The number of runs a team has scored in a game.

platter. Home plate.

play ball. What the umpire yells to begin a game.

play catch. To throw a baseball back and forth.

player. Slang for someone who excels at the game of baseball.

play for keeps. Term for players or teams that compete hard and have a great desire to win.

play to win. Term for players or teams that compete hard and have a great desire to win.

playing .500 ball. A team that wins the same number of games as they lose.

playing catch up. When a team falls behind and is trying to get back into the game.

playing like gangbusters. Term for a player or team that is playing hard and doing well.

playing out the string. When a team that is out of contention for a pennant or championship plays the last few games of a season.

plowed. To get run over by a base runner; usually happens to the catcher.

plugs. Name for the rubber pieces that fit into the base holes when the bases are removed; plugs keep dirt from getting into the holes.

plug the gap. To hit the ball in a gap.

plummet. When a team is dropping fast in the standings.

plunge. When a team is dropping fast in the standings.

plunked. Slang for being hit by a pitch.

plyos. Short for plyometrics; a type of strength and conditioning program consisting of leaping, jumping, and explosive movements.

PO. Abbreviation for putouts.

pole. Slang for a baseball bat.

poles. When players run from foul pole to foul pole near or on the outfield warning track for physical conditioning.

polished. Term for a smooth, well-taught player in the fundamentals of the game.

pond scum. A not so affectionate name for the New York Mets used by the St. Louis Cardinals fans in the middle of the 1980's and in 2000.

PONY. Abbreviation for Protecting Our Nation's Youth; baseball leagues for players ages five through eighteen.

pool play. Refers to the preliminary bracket of a tournament where teams play a round robin format in hopes of finishing first or second and earning the right to advance to the double elimination finals round.

pop. Slang for a lot of power.

popcorn arm. A weak throwing arm.

pop gun. Slang for a player with a weak-throwing arm.

pop off. To talk trash.

popped. Term meaning 1) a ball hit very hard, or 2) a batter struck by a pitch.

popped him up. When a pitcher gets a batter to hit a pop fly.

pop time. Term for the time it takes for a catcher to throw to second base on a stolen base attempt; from the catcher's mitt to the fielder's glove.

position # 1. The pitcher.

position # 2. The catcher.

position # 3. The first baseman.

position # 4. The second baseman.

position # 5. The third baseman.

position # 6. The shortstop.

position # 7. The left fielder.

position # 8. The center fielder.

position # 9. The right fielder.

pounder. A pitcher who throws hard and frequently aims in on the hands.

pound the baseball. To hit the baseball very hard.

pour it on. When a team intentionally runs up the score on an opponent.

powder river. Slang for a pitch thrown very hard.

P

power alleys. Term for left-center and right-center field.

powered. To hit a ball very hard.

power sinker. A breaking ball that is quick and breaks downward, like a slider.

pray for rain. When a team is losing they may want a rain out to stop the game.

press. Term meaning 1) to be tense or anxious when playing the game, or 2) the news media.

pressure cooker. A close game filled with anxiety and stress.

pretender. A team that at one point appeared to be a contender to win their division or league but folded.

pretty boy. A player who is more concerned about his image than playing the game hard.

pro coverage. Refers to the time after the amateur draft when many major league area scouts begin to cover minor league games and players for possible trades.

p-rod. Slang for a hard hit ball.

promoted. To be moved up a level in professional baseball.

promotion. The act of moving a player up a level in professional baseball.

prospect. A young player who is pro-jected to be very good.

protection. When a great hitter has a good hitter batting behind him,

thereby allowing him to see more good pitches to hit.

protect the plate. Encouragement yelled at a batter so he will not get called out on a third strike.

psyche job. Term for when a player's performance is hindered because he is 'psyched out' by the other team.

pug mitt. An old style catcher's mitt that is round and has no break in it.

pulled the right strings. Term for when a manager or coach made a good decision.

pull hitter. A batter who tends to pull the ball the majority of the time he hits.

pulling the strings. When a manager or head coach is making good strategic decisions.

pull off the ball. Term for when a batter's momentum goes away from home plate when he swings; usually caused by a batter moving his head away from the plate.

pull out of the fire. Term meaning 1) to stop a rally, or 2) to win a game after being behind by a lot of runs.

pull the string. To throw a change-up pitch.

pull the trigger. 1) to swing the bat, or 2) phrase yelled at an umpire so he will make a desirable call.

pumper. A fastball.

pumpin' gas. When a pitcher is throwing very hard.

punch. Slang term for power.

punch a hole in that mask. Derogatory saying yelled at an umpire to imply that they are visually challenged.

punch and judy hitter. A hitter who hits weak ground balls and soft fly balls most of the time.

punched. When a ball is hit fairly hard.

punch out. To be called out looking.

punked. To be shown up by another player.

purpose pitch. Refers to a pitch that is high and tight on a batter; meant to send a message to the other team; often thrown in retaliation for one of the pitcher's teammates getting knocked down.

push bunt. A bunt that gets past the pitcher and goes directly toward the second baseman.

pushing a piano. Expression describing a slow runner.

put a charge into one. Hit a ball very hard.

put a spanking on it. Hit a ball hard.

put a tent on that circus. Phrase used 1) when a team plays sloppy baseball and looks like a bunch of clowns on the field, or 2) after a team makes a series of errors.

put a tourniquet on that bleeder. Slang expression inferring that a hit was a bleeder.

put him on his seat. Term for when a pitcher throws a knockdown pitch at a batter.

put him on the ground. Term for when a pitcher throws a knockdown pitch at a batter.

put it out of reach. To score so many runs that the other team cannot come back to win.

put on the brakes. When a player stops suddenly.

put out the fire. To stop a rally.

put out. When a defensive player records an out.

put together. Slang for a player with a great physique.

put up some numbers. When a player has produced great statistics.

P

qualifier. A prospective student-athlete who meets the academic qualifications to be eligible to compete in intercollegiate athletics.

quality start. A good pitching performance, generally thought of as pitching a minimum of six innings and allowing three or less earned runs in a nine-inning game.

quarter. A nickname for number twenty-five.

quarterback. Term for a catcher.

quarter slider. A spinning slider that does not spin very tightly, showing a circle the size of a quarter to the batter.

quench the flames. When a relief pitcher enters a game and stops a rally.

question mark turn. Term for a turn that a base runner makes, between home and first base, when he recognizes that the ball is in the outfield.

quick pitch. Term for 1) a pitcher who works at a faster pace than the batters like, or 2), a pitcher who does not come to a discern-able pause while pitching out of a stretch.

quiet period. The period of time when coaches are permitted to make in-person recruiting contacts, but only on a college campus.

quit beggin'. Phrase yelled at people who constantly yell at the umpires and beg for calls to go their way.

Quiz Picture #15

R. Abbreviation for runs or runs allowed.

rabbit. A player who can run very fast.

rabbit ball. Term for a ball that goes a long way when hit.

rabbit ears. Slang for an umpire who listens to the fans, coaches, and players too much, instead of concentrating on his job.

radar gun. A device that measures the velocity of a pitch.

rag. Word meaning 1) to talk trash, or 2) the cloth used to apply pine tar to a bat.

rag arm. Slang for a pitcher who lacks arm strength.

rainmaker. A fly ball that is hit very high.

rake. To hit well.

rally. A productive inning for the offense in which multiple runs are scored.

rally caps. Refers to a superstitious ritual for good luck in a tight game, where baseball caps are worn backwards or inside out to bring luck.

rally killer. Term for a player who chokes or does not perform well in an important situation.

ran into a buzz saw. Term meaning that a team lost to a very tough team.

rapid fire. When a series of balls are hit hard.

rattle the bats. Expression yelled to try to get a team to start hitting the ball.

RBI. Abbreviation for 1) runs batted in, and 2) Revitalizing Baseball in the Inner cities.

read. When a base runner, while taking his lead off of a base, quickly recognizes if the ball is hit, taken, or thrown in the dirt.

recalled. Term for a player called up to the major leagues from the minor leagues.

receiver. A catcher.

recipe for disaster. Phrase used to describe a play or action that could lead to bad things happening for a team.

red flagged. When a player is cut from a team, a red flag is hung in his locker.

red light. When a player does not have the manager's approval to swing at a pitch or steal a base on his own.

red shirt. Term for when a player, usually during his first year of college, sits out and does not compete in order to maintain four years of eligibility.

reel mower. The type of mower that produces the stripes on the grass of a baseball field.

rehab. Short for rehabilitation; when a player is recovering from an injury.

rehab assignment. When a player who is recovering from an injury starts playing again, often at a lower level of competition.

reign. Term for the length of time a team is defending its championship.

relaxed stance. Refers to a catcher's stance when there are no runners on base or when the count is not three balls, or two strikes, or full.

released. When a player is let go from a team or an organization.

release point. Term for the point in the throwing motion where a player lets go of the baseball.

relic. Slang for a very old ballpark.

relief man. A pitcher from the bullpen who enters a game after

the starting pitcher or another pitcher is removed.

relief pitcher. A pitcher from the bullpen who enters a game after the starting pitcher or another pitcher is removed.

repertoire. Term for an assortment of pitches that a pitcher can throw.

rescue. Slang for a save.

reserve clause. This rule bound a player to the team that held his contract forever; this clause was found to be illegal in the 1960's and 1970's when free agency began.

retaliation. When a pitcher hits an opponent's batter with a pitch as revenge for one of his teammates getting hit.

retire. When a player ends his baseball career.

retire the side. When the defense records the third out of an inning.

retro. Refers to the trend in major league baseball to build new ballparks that architecturally look like parks of old.

revert back to your old habits. When a player starts to go back to an old, and usually incorrect, way of doing things.

rhubarb. A fight between players on two opposing teams.

ribbies. Slang for runs batted in.

rib eyes. Slang for RBI's (runs batted

in).

ride one outta here. To hit a home run.

ride the pine. Term for a player who sits on the bench and doesn't get to play.

riding through balance. Refers to a pitcher who lets his momentum move towards home plate before he reaches a solid balance point in his delivery.

rifle. A strong throwing arm.

rifle arm. Term for a player with a strong throwing arm.

rifleman. A player with a very strong throwing arm.

right back where it came from. To hit the ball right back at the pitcher.

right down Broadway. A pitch thrown right down the middle.

right down central. A pitch thrown right down the middle.

right down Peachtree. A pitch thrown right down the middle.

right down the shoot. A pitch thrown right down the middle.

right man…right spot. Encouragement yelled at a batter to help build his confidence.

right on the chalk. A ball that lands right on the foul line.

right on the money. When a fielder makes an extraordinary accurate throw.

right the ship. To get things going in the right direction.

right through the wickets. A ball that goes right between a fielder's legs.

righty. A right-handed player.

ring 'em up and sit 'em down. Phrase used after a strike out.

ring him up. When a pitcher gets an out on a third strike.

rival. A team's special opponent; another team with whom an intense history of tight games and a general dislike exists.

rivalry. When two teams have an intense history of tight games and general dislike for one another.

roadrunner. A player who can run very fast.

road trip. A number of consecutive games away from home.

rock and fire. Term meaning to wind up and throw the ball hard.

rocked. When a pitcher gets hit hard.

rocker step. Term for the part of a pitcher's mechanics when he takes his initial step back.

rocket. A ball that is hit very hard.

rocket arm. A player who possesses an extremely strong arm.

rocket launcher. Term for a player who hits the ball a very long way.

rocking chair. Term for 1) the third base umpire on a four-man crew,

R

or 2) a pitching philosophy where the location of the pitches alternates from inside to outside to inside and so on, helping to keep the batter off balance.

roll it over. To turn a double play.

roll it up. To turn a double play.

roll up cage. A batting cage that is placed at home plate during batting practice.

rookie. A first year player at each different level of baseball.

Rookie ball. Term for 1) the lowest level of the minor leagues, or 2) a simulated game of baseball using an ATEC Rookie pitching machine to throw the pitches.

rookie mistake. Term used to describe a first year player's mistake that probably occurred as a result of his lack of experience.

roster. A listing of all of the players on a team.

rotation. The order in which a baseball team's starting pitchers start games.

rotisserie. Name for a type of fantasy baseball.

roto. Abbreviation for rotisserie league; fantasy baseball.

roughed up. When a pitcher's pitches get hit very hard.

rounders. Refers to an early version of baseball played in the 1800's.

roundhouse curve. Term for a big, slow-breaking curveball.

round tripper. A home run.

rout. A lop-sided, blow out game.

rover. Term for a coach in professional baseball who travels around to different teams within an organization to teach various fundamentals of the game.

roving hitting instructor. A coach in professional baseball who travels around to different teams within an organization to teach the fundamentals of hitting.

roving pitching instructor. A coach in professional baseball who travels around to different teams within an organization to teach the fundamentals of pitching.

ROY. Abbreviation for rookie of the year.

RPF. Abbreviation for relief failures.

RPI. Abbreviation for ratings percentage index.

rubber. The white pitching plate on the pitcher's mound.

rubber arm. Term meaning 1) a pitcher who seldom gets a sore arm, or 2) a player who has a weak throwing arm, in youth baseball slang.

rubber game. The third game in a series that is tied at one game each.

rubber necking. Term for a player who is watching a play instead of getting his job done.

Rule 5 draft. In December, during major league baseball's winter meetings, teams that have room on their 40-man roster can select unprotected players for $50,000 compensation. The selected player must stay on the 40-man roster for the whole season or be offered back to the original team for $25,000, unless a deal is made.

run. Term meaning 1) to get good movement on a pitch, 2) to be ejected from a game, or 3) the basic unit of scoring in baseball.

run and gun. Refers to an era in baseball when there were a lot of stolen bases and the play was very aggressive.

rung up. To strike out looking.

run him out there. Phrase for when a pitcher is given the ball and sent out to the mound.

runner up. A second place team.

running in place. Term used for 1) a team that is playing .500 baseball, or 2) a very slow runner.

running too long in the same spot. Slang for a very slow runner.

run off the plate. When a pitcher throws a ball high and tight.

run producers. A team's top RBI guys; usually the three, four, and five hole hitters.

run support. The number of runs a team scores when each particular pitcher is pitching.

run the table. When a team wins out against a particular team and wins the remainder of their scheduled games.

run their mouth. To talk trash.

rushing. When a pitcher lets his momentum move towards home plate before he reaches a solid balance point in his delivery.

Ruthian. Refers to a player putting up great power numbers.

R

Quiz Picture #16

60 time. The amount of time it takes a player to run 60 yards; 60 yards is the standard timed sprint length in baseball.

S. Abbreviation for saves.

sack. A base.

sacks are jammed. Slang for the bases are loaded.

saddled with the loss. When a pitcher is given a loss.

safed him. Term umpires use meaning to call someone safe.

safety. Term for 1) a hit, or 2) a type of squeeze bunt.

salami. Slang for a grand slam.

Sally League. A mid A league within minor league baseball.

salty. Slang for a very good player or team.

salvage. When a team wins the final game in a series after losing the earlier ones.

same spot...different location. Phrase yelled at an inconsistent umpire who has just called two identical pitches differently.

sandwich pick. Refers to draft picks that occur between the first and second rounds of the major league baseball amateur draft.

sat down. The number of batters a pitcher has gotten out.

saucer. Slang for home plate.

sawed off. To get jammed.

SB. Abbreviation for stolen bases.

SB%. Abbreviation for stolen base percentage (stolen bases divided by [stolen bases + caught stealing] = stolen base percentage).

scamper. To run very fast.

scoot. To run very fast.

scorched. A ball that is hit very hard.

scoring position. When a base runner is on second or third base.

scraps. Term for 1) weak stuff thrown by a pitcher, or 2) fights.

scratch out a run. To work hard to get a run.

scratch out a win. To work hard to get a win.

screamer. A hard hit ball.

screwball. Term for 1) a player who is very unusual; can be good for a team because he can keep the team loose, or 2) a type of breaking ball that curves the opposite direction as a regular curveball.

scrub. A seldom-used reserve player.

scud. A ball hit very hard.

scuff brothers. Name for brothers Phil and Joe Niekro.

scuffle. A fight between players on two opposing teams.

seal the deal. The end of a game or a point in a game when the outcome has been established.

secondary. An aggressive two-shuffle lead off by a base runner.

second cleanup. The eighth batter in the line up.

second-guess. To debate or criticize a manager or head coach's decisions.

second sacker. The second baseman.

secret weapon. A player who is a decent player but is not very well known.

seed. A hard hit ball.

seedling. A hard hit ball.

seeing eye single. A softly hit ball that barely gets through the infield.

seesaw game. A game that has a number of lead changes.

see ya. Term yelled when a home run is hit.

selection committee. The committee at the NCAA that selects what teams will play in the post-season tournament.

sellers. Teams that decide by the July 31st trade deadline that they are out of the pennant race and try to trade high-priced veterans to dump salary or trade players who will be unaffordable free agents at the end of the year.

sellout. When all of the available tickets for a game are sold.

send a message. Term for a pitch that is high and tight, sometimes thrown in retaliation for one of the pitcher's teammates getting knocked down.

send in the cleanup crew. Phrase meaning to start using relief pitchers because a team is getting beaten badly.

senior circuit. The National League.

senior loop. The National League.

Senior sign. When a player signs a professional contract after his Senior year of college.

sense of urgency. When players on a team that is on the verge of falling out of the pennant race realize that they must start playing better or their hopes of a championship will be over.

sent out. Sent to the minor leagues.

September call up. A player called up on or after September 1st, the date when major league teams can expand their rosters.

serve it up. To give up a home run.

serving up meat. A pitcher with ineffective stuff.

set. A series.

set the table. When a player gets on base so that the team's power hitters can drive him in.

set the tone. Term used when an important play early in a game has a big impact on the rest of the contest.

set up man. A middle reliever who pitches before the team's closer comes in.

seven hole. The seventh batter in the batting order.

seventh inning stretch. Refers to the tradition of standing up and stretching before the home team bats in the seventh inning.

SF. Abbreviation for sacrifice fly.

SH. Abbreviation for sacrifice hits and sacrifice hits allowed.

shag. To chase batting practice balls.

shag bag. A piece of equipment used to collect shagged balls.

shagger. A person who chases batting practice balls.

shake it off. Encouragement yelled to a teammate to not let a mis-

take bother him.

shake yourself blue. Phrase yelled at an umpire to suggest that he needs to do a better job concentrating.

shellacked. Term for 1) a pitcher whose pitches get hit very hard, or 2) a batter who hits a ball very hard.

shelled. A pitcher whose pitches are getting hit very hard.

shine ball. Term for a ball that a pitcher has put spit or some other foreign substance on to get it to sink in an unnatural way.

SHO. Abbreviation for shutouts.

shoestring catch. When a fielder catches a ball near his shoes, just before it hits the ground.

shoe-top liner. A line drive no higher than the top of a fielder's shoe.

shoot the gap. When a ball is hit to the wall between two outfielders.

shop him around. When a team's management talks to other teams in hopes of trading a player.

short and sweet. Instruction yelled to a batter to remind him to take a shorter stride and a more compact swing.

short armer. A player who short arms the ball when they throw.

shot. A hard hit ball.

show a glove. Term for when a first baseman plays right behind a base runner instead of holding him on.

showboat. A player who shows off and is known as a hot dog.

showdown. A much anticipated game between two formidable opponents.

showing their true colors. When a player or team begins to play at their usual performance level after a hot streak.

show move. When a pitcher makes a soft throw to first base with a runner on.

show no emotion. Advice yelled to a player, usually a pitcher, who shows his emotions when adversity happens; a pitcher who restrains his emotions adheres to the etiquette of baseball.

shuffle the deck. When manager or head coach changes the usual batting order to try and get more productivity from his offense.

shutdown mode. Term for 1) when players or an entire team quits playing hard in a game or at the end of a season, or 2) when a pitcher or a pitching staff keeps their opponents from scoring.

shut it down. When a relief pitcher comes into a game and gets a save.

shut out. A game where the opposing team does not score a run.

sick. Slang for a nasty pitch.

side is retired. When three outs are made by the defense in an inning.

sidewinder. Term for a side-arm pitcher.

signability. The likelihood that a college or professional organization can sign a player.

signal caller. A catcher.

signs of life. When a team exhibits resiliency and starts to play better baseball after a cold streak.

silk. Term for a defensive player who is smooth and fluid in his actions.

single marker. Scoring one run in an inning.

sinker. A type of breaking ball that literally sinks when it gets near the plate.

sinkerball. A pitch that sinks when it gets near home plate.

sinkerballer. A pitcher who relies heavily on his sinkerball to get batters out.

sinkerball pitcher. A pitcher who relies heavily on his sinkerball to get batters out.

sinking life. Term for a pitch that sinks at the plate.

sit and get hit. Refers to a drill for catchers that starts with them in the position they are suppose to be in to block balls, and then one ball at a time is thrown so it bounces and hits the player.

sit down in your seat. Phrase yelled at an opposing batter when he strikes out.

sitting on a curveball. When a batter is looking for a curveball to hit.

sitting on a fastball. When a batter is looking for a fastball to hit.

sittin' pretty. Term used when a team is in great shape to win a game or a championship.

situational hitting. Refers to hitting according to what the game situation dictates while following the fundamentals of baseball.

six hole. The sixth batter in the batting order.

sizzler. Term for a baseball that is hit very hard.

skid. A losing streak.

skies one. When a player hits a high fly ball.

skillet. Term for 1) a baseball field on a very hot day, or 2) a poor fielder who is said to have skillet hands, implying that he is actually fielding with a real skillet in his glove because of the way the ball bounces out of it.

skipper. A manager or head coach of a baseball team.

skirmish. A fight.

skully. Term for a catcher's protective helmet.

slab. Slang for the pitcher's rubber.

slacker. A lazy, underachieving player.

slam the door. When a relief pitcher comes into the game and keeps the other team from winning.

slap hitter. A hitter who tries to slap the ball around to all fields; usually a player who possesses excellent speed.

slap tag. When a fielder catches the ball and slaps the glove on the runner to tag him out.

slash. A play where the batter fakes a bunt and then pulls the bat back to swing; this play is normally used when the defense has a bunt coverage called.

sleeper. An underrated team that has the potential to sneak up on a favored team and beat them.

sleepover series. Term for a two-game series in the major leagues.

sleeves. The long-sleeved shirt required to be worn by most pitchers to keep their arms warm.

SLG. Abbreviation for slugging percentage (total bases divided by at bats = slugging percentage).

slice. When a ball is hit down the foul line of the opposite field.

sliced. A batted ball that curves toward the foul line of the opposite field.

slide. Term for 1) a losing streak, or 2) a way a base runner approaches a base to avoid a tag by scooting on his butt, feet first, or on his belly, head first.

slider. A type of breaking pitch that sinks down and away or down and in to batters.

slim pickins. When very few runs are scored on a pitcher at the top of his game.

slinging hash. Slang for a hard thrown pitch.

slip pitch. Slang for various types of off-speed pitches.

slow afoot. A player who runs slow.

slow as Christmas. Term used to describe a very slow runner.

slowballer. A pitcher who throws the ball very slow.

slug bunt. A play where the batter fakes a bunt and then pulls the bat back to swing; this play is normally used when the defense has a bunt coverage called.

slugfest. Term for a very high scoring baseball game.

slugger. A great power hitter.

slump. A period of time during the season when a player or a team is struggling and performing below average.

slurve. A breaking pitch that is half slider and half curve.

small ball. Strategic emphasis on bunting, stealing, and the hit and run; trying to play for one run at a time.

small market team. Term for a major league team that is located in a small television market limiting the amount of revenue that can be generated through broadcasts; this, among other factors, helps to determine payroll for the teams.

smash. A baseball that is hit very hard.

smoke. A hard pitched ball.

smoked. A baseball that is hit very hard.

smoker. Term for 1) a hard-hit ball, or 2) a hard-thrown pitch.

snag. Term meaning to catch a ball that is difficult to get to.

snap throw. A quick pick-off move to first base by a left-handed pitcher.

snare. To catch a baseball.

snatch. To steal a base.

sneaky fast. Term for a pitcher who throws harder than it appears.

sniper. An expression yelled when a player falls down or trips for no apparent reason.

snow cone. A catch made with the ball showing at the top of the glove.

snowman. A name for number eight.

snubbed. To barely foul tip a pitch.

snuff out a rally. When a relief pitcher enters a game and stops a rally.

SO. Abbreviation for strikeouts.

socked. A ball that is hit very hard.

soft hands. A fielder who appears to have a soft glove will keep his elbow relaxed so the glove gives with the ball and helps achieve the look of soft hands.

soft receiver. A catcher who has good hands and makes receiving pitches appear easy.

sold. When one team pays money to another team to buy the services of a player.

sold him. When a player makes a play that sells an out to an umpire.

solo job. A home run with no one on base.

Sophomore campaign. A player's second season.

Sophomore jinx. An expression used to describe players that have a bad year after a great rookie season.

South Atlantic League. A mid A league within minor league baseball.

Southern League. A minor league baseball AA league.

southpaw. A left-handed player.

Southsiders. Term for the Chicago White Sox.

spanked. Term that means 1) to be beaten badly, 2) to hit the ball very hard.

sparkling play. Expression used to describe a great play.

spark plug. A player who gets on base in front of a team's power hitters.

spear the ball. To catch the ball while on the run.

spectators. Fans who watch baseball games.

speed burner. A player who can run very fast.

speed demon. A player who can run very fast.

speed merchant. A player who can run very fast.

speedster. A player who can run very fast.

spiked curve. A curveball grip where one fingernail digs into a seam like a knuckleball grip.

spike move. A quick step-off and look move, usually to first base, by a right-handed pitcher.

spitball. When a pitcher puts spit or some other foreign substance on the ball to get it to move in an unnatural way.

spitter. A spitball.

split. Term that means 1) to win a game and lose a game in a doubleheader, or 2) a split-finger fastball or forkball.

splity. A split-finger fastball or forkball.

spray chart. A statistical graph that shows where each batter hits the ball.

spray hitter. A player who hits the ball to all fields.

springboard to success. Term for a performance by a team or a player that leads to future success.

squeaker. Term for 1) a close game, or 2) a softly hit ball.

squeezed. When an umpire reduces his strike zone against a team.

squelch the rally. To stop a rally.

squibber. A softly hit, spinning baseball.

squirter. A softly hit ball.

squish the bug. A youth league instructional term for pivoting the back foot during the follow through while hitting.

SRO. Abbreviation for standing room only.

staff. All of the pitchers on a baseball team; short for pitching staff.

staff ace. The best pitcher on a baseball team.

staked to a lead. When a pitcher's team gets ahead early in a game and gives the pitcher a momentary lead.

stakes are high. Phrase used to describe a very important game, such as a regular season game in the stretch drive or a playoff game.

standing "O". A standing ovation.

standings. A chart that displays a team's wins, losses, and the number of games they are in front or behind in their division.

stand up guy. A player who admits to his mistakes.

stanza. An inning.

star. A great player who receives a lot of publicity.

stave off elimination. When a team avoids being eliminated from a pennant race or tournament.

stay afloat. When a team barely remains in a pennant race or above the .500 mark.

stay back. Encouragement yelled at a batter to not lunge while swinging.

stay within yourself. Reminder to a player not to try and play beyond his capabilities.

steady diet of fastballs. When a pitcher throws a batter mostly fastballs.

steady diet of off speed stuff. When a pitcher throws a batter mostly curveballs and changeups.

steaks. Slang term that originates from rib eyes (RBIs or runs batted in).

steaks on the table. Term for when potential RBI's are in scoring position; steak comes from a slang term that originates from rib eyes (RBIs or runs batted in), while table refers to the bases.

stellar performance. A great performance.

step and slap. A youth league instructional term for striding and lunging while hitting a ball.

step and throw. Instruction yelled to a pitcher when he fields a ball and throws to a base.

step bunt. A bunt that gets past the pitcher and goes directly toward the second baseman; sometimes called a push bunt.

step in the bucket. Expression for when a batter's front foot steps away from the plate while the pitch is on its way.

step into it. Encouragement given to a batter to hit the ball hard.

step it up. Encouragement given to a player to play better and harder.

stepping-stone. Term for a coaching job that gives a coach experience for a bigger and better paying job in the future.

step up. To deliver in a clutch situation.

sterling performance. Phrase used to describe a superbly played game.

stick. A baseball bat.

stick a fork in him…he's done. Expression used when a pitcher is tiring.

sticks. A name for number eleven.

stiff. Term for a bad baseball player.

sting. Term for 1) the feeling a fielder gets when they catch the ball in the palm, or 2) the feeling a batter gets when he gets jammed or hits the ball on the end of the bat.

sting the baseball. To hit the ball very hard.

stone hands. Term for a poor fielder who tends to have a lot of balls bounce off his glove.

stopper. A team's closer.

stop the bleeding. When a pitcher stops a rally.

storied franchise. Term for a franchise rich in tradition that is used to winning.

storied program. A program rich in tradition that is used to winning.

straighten it out. Encouragement yelled to a batter after a long foul ball.

straight up the shoot. A pop fly that goes straight up in the air and comes down right at home plate.

straightens him up. When a pitch is thrown high and tight to back the batter off of the plate.

stranded. When runners are left on base.

stretch. When a fielder steps and reaches out as far as possible with his glove to catch a ball and record an out.

stretch drive. The last part of the baseball season when the pennant races heat up.

stretch run. The last part of a baseball season when a division or league championship is decided.

strike 'em out, throw 'em out. A play where the batter strikes out and the base runner is thrown out by the catcher to complete a double play.

string a few together. To get consecutive wins, hits, or runs.

stroke. Term meaning 1) to swing a bat, or 2) to hit the ball well.

strong suit. The strengths of a player or a team.

stud. Slang for a great baseball player.

stuff. Term for all of a pitcher's pitches.

stumbled out of the gates. Phrase describing a team that gets off to a slow start.

stymied. When a pitcher or pitchers shut down a team on any given day.

Subway Series. Refers to the 2000 World Series between the New York Yankees and the New York Mets.

suck it up. Encouragement yelled at a player to get tough.

suffered the loss. When a pitcher is credited with a loss.

Sultan of Swat. Nickname for Babe Ruth.

summoned from the pen. When a manager calls for a relief pitcher to come into a ballgame.

Sunday hop. When a fielder gets an ideal bounce to help him get the runner out.

SUP. Abbreviation for run support.

superstar. A famous player who receives a lot of publicity and makes a lot of money.

SV. Abbreviation for saves.

SVO. Abbreviation for save opportunities.

swap. A trade between two teams.

swat. To hit the ball.

sweep. When one team wins all of the games in a series with another team.

sweeper. Term for a slow curveball that sweeps across the strike zone, usually thrown by a lefty.

sweet play. A good play.

sweet spot. Term for 1) the best part of the bat to hit the ball, or 2) the fat part of the bat close to the trademark.

sweet swing. A smooth, powerful swing.

swinging a hot bat. Term for a player who has recently been hitting the ball well.

swinging a log. To swing a large wooden bat.

swinging a twig. To swing a small wooden bat.

swinging for the downs. To try and hit a home run by swinging as hard as possible.

swinging the hardwood. To swing a wooden bat.

swinging the plank. To swing a wooden bat.

swinging the timber. To swing a wooden bat.

s

swing the ax. To swing a baseball bat.

swing the gavel. To swing a baseball bat.

swipe. Term meaning to steal a base.

swipe tag. When a fielder catches the ball and swipes the glove at the runner to tag him out.

switch hitter. A player who can bat right-handed or left-handed.

synthetic surface. Astroturf.

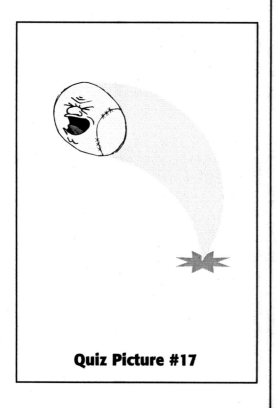

Quiz Picture #17

Quiz Picture #18

2B. Abbreviation for both a double and a second baseman.

2 runner. A runner who possesses average speed.

3B. Abbreviation for both a triple and a third baseman.

3 runner. A runner who possesses below-average speed.

10/5 man. A major league player who has played ten years in the big leagues and five years with the same team; has a say in trade matters.

12/6. Term for the proper spin on a baseball thrown by a non-pitcher; 12/6 refers to the visual image of the ball spinning end-over-end, from the 12 at the top of a clock and the six at the bottom.

20/20 ball. A seeing-eye single.

25-man roster. The number of players allowed on a regular season major league roster.

30-30 man. A player who hits 30 home runs and steals 30 bases in the same season.

31. Term for a pick-off move in which a right-handed pitcher fakes a throw to third base and then quickly looks toward first base hoping to catch that base runner off the base.

table setter. A player who gets on base so that the team's power hitters can drive him in.

tagged. A ball that is hit very hard.

tagged with the loss. When a pitcher is credited with a loss.

tailed off. When a team or a player who is in the midst of a hot streak begins to cool off.

tailor made double play. A ball hit perfectly to an infielder so he can begin an easy double play.

take a hack. Phrase yelled at a batter before or after he swings the bat very hard.

take a little off, put a little on. Instruction yelled to a pitcher to remind him to mix the speeds of his pitches to keep the batter off balance.

take an 0'fer. When a player does not get any hits in a game or series.

T

take a ride on that one. Term used after a home run is hit.

take a seat. Expression yelled at an opposing player after he makes an out.

take him out. Instruction yelled at a base runner to remind him to make an aggressive slide, particularly at second base, to break up a double play.

take one for the team. Expression yelled at a batter suggesting that he allow himself to get hit by a pitch so he can get to first.

take the field. When players run onto the field, ready to play.

take the hill. When a pitcher gets on the mound, ready to pitch.

take the mound. When a pitcher gets on the mound, ready to pitch.

take your time. Instructions yelled at a batter to remind him to not let the pitcher quick-pitch him.

taking all the way. When a batter doesn't try to swing at any pitches until the count is three balls and two strikes.

talk smack. To talk trash.

tally. Slang for a run.

tamp. A piece of equipment that is used to flatten out and level dirt and clay in the batter's box and pitcher's mound areas.

tandem relay. When a ball is hit to the wall and the shortstop and second baseman both go out into the outfield to be the cutoff men.

tanked it. Term meaning 1) to purposely make an error, or 2) to purposely hit poorly.

tanker. Term for 1) a bad pitcher, 2) to purposely make an error, or 3) to purposely hit poorly.

tap. A ball hit very soft.

tape measure job. A home run hit very far.

tapper. A very softly hit ground ball.

target. When a catcher holds up his mitt to show the pitcher where he wants him to throw the ball.

target, turn, stick. Refers to a technique used by catchers to prepare to receive a pitch; give the target, turn and break the mitt by relaxing the wrist downward, and stick the pitch where it's caught.

tarp. A tarpaulin is put on the infield when it rains to keep the field from getting wet.

tater. A home run.

TBBQ. Short for the four similarities between hitting and pitching that need to be carried out to give a player a good chance to succeed: he must 1) stay tall, 2) balanced, 3) back, and 4) quiet; refers to body control and physiological efficiency.

TBF. Abbreviation for total batters faced.

TC. Abbreviation for total chances.

team chemistry. Refers to the way teammates get along with each other on and off the field.

team to beat. Term for the team that is favored to win the league or division.

tell that one goodbye. Phrase yelled after a home run is hit.

ten percenter. A lazy, underachieving player, who usually arrives at the last minute and leaves as soon as practice is over.

Texas League. A minor league baseball AA league.

Texas leaguer. Term for a softly hit fly ball that often drops in front of an outfielder.

that ball was yellow. Phrase used to describe a hard hit ball.

that dog'll hunt. Term used by some Southern players after a base hit or run batted in.

that run means nothing. Term yelled to players referring to the non-tying or go-ahead run on base.

that's a winner. Refers to the famous call from hall of fame announcer Jack Buck after the St. Louis Cardinals clinched a game.

that's garbage. Phrase 1) yelled when a player on one team commits an unsportsmanlike act towards a player on the other team, or 2) yelled at an umpire after a very bad call.

that's the ole pepper. An old saying yelled as encouragement to a pitcher to throw hard.

the ball will find him. Expression that means if a team is trying to hide a poor fielder the ball will find him anyway.

the Bambino. Babe Ruth.

the basement. Last place.

the black. The outer edge of home plate that is black.

the BOB. Refers to Bank One Ballpark; home of the Arizona Diamondbacks.

the book. A mythical 'book' that possesses the typical or traditional way to play the game or carry out strategy.

the box. A listing of statistics for a baseball game; short for box score.

the break. The major league baseball all-star break.

the bureau. The major league baseball scouting bureau.

the cellar. The place where the last place team resides.

the Clearinghouse. The place that a high school student, after his junior year, sends his high school transcripts, along with his ACT and/or SAT scores so as to be deemed eligible to participate in NCAA intercollegiate athletics; officially called the NCAA Initial-Eligibility Clearinghouse.

T

the code. The unwritten rules of etiquette and respect in the game of baseball, i.e., don't bunt or steal with a big lead; don't bunt in the late innings to break up a no hitter; don't talk to, or sit by a pitcher while he has a late inning no-hitter going; there is great debate as to exactly what is permissible and what is not, since the rules are unwritten and merely an "understanding."

the count. The number of balls, strikes, and outs at a given time.

the craft. A crafty pitcher, usually a left hander, who throws slow and depends on changeups, curveballs, and movement on the ball to get batters out.

the Cy Young. The award given to the "best" pitcher in the American and National leagues.

the damage is done. Phrase used after the defense retires the side but not before the other teams offense had a big inning.

the express. A fastball.

thefts. Stolen bases.

the garden. The outfield.

the gun. A radar gun that measures the velocity of a pitch.

the hall. The major league baseball hall of fame.

The Heat Is On. The slogan and theme song for the 1985 National League champion St. Louis Cardinals.

the house that Ruth built. Yankee Stadium.

the Jake. Jacobs field; home of the Cleveland Indians.

the Jugs. A type of radar gun that measures the velocity of a pitch at the release point of a pitch.

the jury's still out. Term that means 1) it remains to be seen if a particular player will develop into a great player, or 2) it remains to be seen if a team will continue their great play.

the lightning. The speed of a team's lineup.

the line. The betting line on a game.

the lot. A baseball field.

the Miracle of Coogan's Bluff. Refers to the legendary home run hit by Bobby Thomson of the New York Giants to beat the Brooklyn Dodgers in the 1951 National League Championship Series; a.k.a. 'the shot heard round the world'; (Coogan's Bluff was the hill above the Giants home field, the Polo Grounds).

the mistake by the lake. Municipal Stadium, former home of the Cleveland Indians.

the next level. The next higher level of baseball above where a player is presently playing; college or pro ball for some high school players, pro ball for some college players.

the ole wholesaler. Slang for a double play.

the other way. To hit the ball to the right side of the field for a right-handed batter and to the left side of the field for a left-handed batter.

the pen. The bullpen.

the plate's not round blue. Derogatory phrase yelled at an umpire who will not call a strike on the corner.

the Ray. A type of radar gun that measures the velocity of a pitch at the home plate area.

the shot heard 'round the world'. The legendary home run hit by Bobby Thomson of the New York Giants to beat the Brooklyn Dodgers in the 1951 National League Championship Series.

the show. Major league baseball.

the small bears. The Chicago Cubs.

the Stick. Candlestick Park; former home of the San Francisco Giants.

the thunder. The power of a team's lineup.

the tool. A tool that cleans out dirt from base holes where the bases go.

the track. A warning track; a non-grassy area near the outfield wall that alerts the outfielders that the wall is near.

the Vet. Veteran Stadium; home of the Philadelphia Phillies.

the whiff. A strike out.

they didn't come to play. Term for a team that plays poorly.

they don't rebuild...they reload. Expression referring to a program rich in tradition that rarely has an off year because their recruiting and signing of players is so strong.

they're dancing in the streets tonight. Refers to a player's home town when he does very well.

third sacker. The third baseman.

three-bagger. A triple.

three depth. When infielders play even with the bag or are on the infield grass to look for a play at the plate.

three hole. The third batter in the batting order.

three in the well. Three outs.

three man crew. An umpiring team where three men umpire a game.

three up...three down. Term used 1) to encourage a pitcher to retire the side in order, or 2) when the offensive team's first three batters make three outs in succession.

throng. A big crowd.

throttled. To be beaten badly.

throw back. Refers to a hard-nosed, gritty player who plays the game for the love of it and not for the money.

throw gas on the fire. A pitcher who comes into the game and makes matters worse.

T

throwing aspirin tablets. Term for when a pitcher is throwing the ball very hard.

throwing bb's. When a pitcher throws the ball very hard and makes the ball look as small as a bb.

throwing darts. A pitcher with pinpoint control.

throwing fire. To throw a baseball very hard.

throwing gas. To throw a baseball very hard.

throwing major hair. Term for a pitcher with exceptionally good stuff.

throwing pellets. When a pitcher throws the ball very hard and makes the ball look as small as a pellet.

throwing Tic Tacs. When a pitcher throws the ball very hard and makes the ball look as small as Tic Tacs.

throw in the towel. To quit.

thrown into the fire. When a player is put into a difficult situation.

throw strikes. Term used to encourage a pitcher to throw strikes.

throw the hands. Instructional advice yelled at batters; a technique of teaching batter's to hit.

thug. A player who lacks self discipline and is a "bad actor".

thumb to thigh, show it to the sky. Instructions for a young pitcher to help promote the proper arm swing while throwing the ball.

thumb to thumb. A technique for fielding a ball; the inside part of both wrists are touching; this contributes to a quicker release and provides a safety factor since the ball will hit the palm of fielder's hand instead of his face.

tilt. A baseball game.

tipping his pitches. When something in a pitcher's action gives a clue to the other team as to what pitch he will throw.

toeing the slab. When a pitcher makes contact with the pitching rubber.

toe the rubber. When a pitcher makes contact with the pitching rubber.

Tommy John surgery. Refers to a type of surgery on the throwing elbow that resurrected Tommy John's career and is very common today.

took something off. Reduced the velocity of a pitch.

tools. Term for 1) catcher's equipment, or 2) player's abilities, including arm strength, hitting for power, hitting for average, fielding ability and running speed.

tools of ignorance. Slang for catcher's equipment.

tools of the trade. Baseball equipment.

top. Refers to the first half of an inning when the visiting team bats.

top half. Refers to the first half of an inning when the visiting team bats.

top of the order. The first, second, and third batters in the batting order.

top of the rotation starter. The pitching ace of the team.

tossed. Term meaning 1) to get thrown out of a game, or 2) to have thrown a baseball.

total team effort. A cliché that many people use to give credit to the entire team for a victory.

totals and highlights in a minute. Phrase that the St. Louis Cardinals' announcers say after a game is over.

touched. Term for a pitch that was hit very hard.

touched it off. Hit a ball very hard.

touch 'em all. Hit a home run.

town ball. Refers to an early version of baseball played in the 1890's.

toy cannon. A very strong throwing arm.

TP. Abbreviation for triple plays.

trade. When teams exchange players.

trade an out for a run. When a team's infielders play back at one depth with a base runner on third base and are willing to give up a run for an out.

trade bait. Term for a player who is being shopped around by his team in the hopes that he may be included in a trade.

trade deadline. July 31 is the official trade deadline, thereby allowing a player to be eligible for the play-offs.

trademark. The burned brand on the sweet spot of a wooden bat.

trading block. Term used to describe the process of clubs trading players.

trainer. A Certified Athletic Trainer who is responsible for the prevention and care of injuries.

trampoline glove. Term for 1) when the ball often bounces out of a fielder's glove, or 2) a fielder who has hard hands.

trap. When a fielder does not catch a ball cleanly because it is lodged against another object.

trash talker. A player who runs his mouth.

treading water. Term for 1) a team that is playing .500 ball, or 2) a team that is barely hanging on in a pennant race.

trial by fire. When an inexperienced player is put into a difficult situation.

trigger. A preparation point in the mechanics of a swing.

triple crown. Term for when player leads his league in batting average, home runs, and runs batted in.

T

true hop. A ground ball that takes normal hops and is easier to field.

tubing. Refers to a conditioning technique using surgical tubing that helps increase strength and flexibility in a player's throwing arm.

tumbler. A forkball or split-finger fastball that bottoms out at the plate.

turnabout is fair play. When a team responds in kind to some action done against them, i.e., a knockdown pitch or a hard slide into second base.

turn a dime. Complete a double play.

turn and burn. Term for a batter who swings as hard as he can almost every pitch.

turned it over. Term for 1) a change-up pitch, or 2) when a team turned a double play.

turn it on. Increase playing intensity.

turn it over. Turn a double play.

turn it up. A double play.

turn on it. To pull the baseball.

turn over the lineup. Term for when the batter in the ninth position gets on base, enabling the leadoff hitter to bat.

turn the page. Phrase yelled at a pitcher who continuously throws to first base.

turn two. To turn a double play.

tussle. Slang for a hard fought game.

twilight of their career. The last few years of a player's career.

twin bill. A doubleheader.

twin killing. A double play.

twirl. To throw a pitch.

two and out. Term describing a team that wins their first tournament game and then is eliminated as a result of a second game loss.

two-bagger. A double.

two depth. When the middle infielders play at double play depth to position themselves to turn a double play.

two hole. The second batter in the batting order.

two in the wagon…one a draggin'. Phrase yelled with two outs and one out to go in an inning.

two in the well. Two outs.

two looker. A pitcher who, while having a base runner on second, looks at the runner twice before pitching the ball.

two-man crew. An umpiring team where two men umpire a game.

two seamer. A type of grip used by a pitcher in which he holds his index and middle fingers on two seams of the baseball.

Uecker seats. Refers to the seats at the top of the stadium.

ugly finder. Term yelled when a hard foul ball goes into the opponent's dugout, implying that the opponents are ugly.

uncle Charlie. Slang for a curve ball.

unconscious. Term for a player when he is on an unbelievable hot streak.

uncorks one. Throws a ball away.

underdog. Term for the team that is predicted to lose a game.

under the gun. A player or coach performing under extreme pressure.

under the lights. To play a night game.

under the weather. A player who plays while sick.

unhitch the trailer. Derogatory phrase yelled at a very slow runner implying that he is running with a trailer hitched to him.

uni. Short for baseball uniform.

uniform. The clothing a baseball player wears during a game.

unintentional intentional walk. A way to avoid pitching to a dangerous hitter while not literally giving him an intentional walk.

unload on one. To hit a ball hard.

unloads. Hits a ball hard.

unsung hero. A player who plays a vital role in a team's success but receives very little notoriety.

up stairs. A pitch high and out of the strike zone.

up start. A player or team that gets out to a surprising start at the beginning of a season.

up the v. Term for a technique used by catchers to block pitches.

up to his old tricks. A player who is performing in his usual way.

upset. When the underdog team beats a favored team.

upsurge. A team that is playing well and makes up ground on the teams ahead of them in the standings.

USABA. United States Amateur Baseball Association; for players ages 11-19.

use your good eye blue. Derogatory term yelled at an umpire to imply that he is half blind.

USSSA. United States Specialty Sports Association; for players ages five to adult.

utility man. A player who can play several different positions.

U

Quiz Picture #19

Quiz Picture #20

V-W

vet. Short for veteran; a player who has played for a long time.

veteran. A player who has played for a long time.

W. Abbreviation for a win or wins.

wait for your pitch. Encouragement yelled at a batter to be patient and swing at a pitch he can hit hard.

wait 'til next year. Phrase used by the fans of ball clubs that didn't win.

waivers. Refers to when a club releases a player in order to find out if any other teams are interested in signing him.

wake up blue. Phrase yelled at an umpire to imply that he was sleeping during a particular call.

wake up call. When something happens that stirs a team into refocusing on the task at hand.

walk off home run. A home run hit by a player on the home team that instantly wins the game.

walk off shot. A game winning hit, usually a home run.

walk's as good as a hit. Encouragement yelled at a batter to just get on base.

walk year. The last year on a player's current contract.

warning track. A non-grassy area near the outfield wall that alerts outfielders that they are near the wall.

warning track power. A term used jokingly when a player hits the ball to the warning track and barely misses a home run.

washed up. A player whose best playing days are behind him.

wash out. A rain out.

wash up. A player whose best playing days are behind him, usually because of age or physical condition.

watched out. To take a call third strike or to strike out looking.

watch your lips. Term yelled so that a hard hit ball doesn't hit someone.

way to battle. Encouragement yelled to a player after battling a pitcher.

way to hang tough. Encouragement given to a player who is playing hard.

We Are Family. The slogan and theme song for the 1979 World Champion Pittsburgh Pirates.

wear it. Encouragement for a batter to get hit by a pitch so he can get on base.

wear the collar. A batter is said to wear this if he has no hits in a game.

wear the horns. Term for a player who did something to lose a game; they are considered the goat and wear the "horns".

we got our hat handed to us. Refers to when a team is beaten badly.

we'll be seeing ya. Phrase used when a home run is hit or a strike-out is recorded.

we need a pitcher…not a belly itcher. A youth league chant yelled at the opposing pitcher.

went fishing. To swing at a ball in the dirt.

went the distance. Pitched a complete game.

went yard. Hit a home run.

west-to-east curveball. A curveball from a left-hander that breaks from left to right.

we've got lift off. Term used after a home run is hit.

what game you watchin' blue? Inference that the umpire is not concentrating on the game he is calling.

what's the count? When a player or coach asks the umpire to confirm the count.

wheel. A type of bunt coverage often used with a runner on second base.

wheel and deal. To trade player(s) to another team in exchange for new players.

wheelhouse. Term for the location in the strike zone where a player has his most power.

wheels. Term for a player who can run fast.

wheels are back on. When a struggling team starts to play better baseball.

wheels are in motion. A critical point in the game when the manager or coach must employ strategy and perhaps make position changes.

wheels are spinning. A critical point in the game when the manager or coach must employ strategy and perhaps make position changes.

wheels came off. When things are going very bad for a baseball team.

wheels fell off. When a team hits a tough spot and things seem to fall apart.

whiffed. To strike out.

whiff prone. Term for a player who is very susceptible to striking out.

WHIP. Abbreviation for (walks + hits divided by innings pitched = WHIP).

whistler. A ball hit very hard.

wicked. Slang for a nasty pitch.

wild card. One American and one National team that earn a trip to the playoffs, even though they do not win their division. They qualify by having the best records of all non-division-winning teams in their leagues.

Williamsport. Williamsport, Pennsylvania, the home of the Little League World Series.

win at all cost. A mindset that attempts to justify any and all actions, including cheating, in order to win a game.

wind blown. A home run that was helped out of the ballpark by the wind.

wind up. The pitching motion of a pitcher when no one is on base.

wing. Term for a player's arm.

Winning Ugly. The slogan for the 1983 West Division Champion Chicago White Sox.

win out. When a team wins all of the remaining games on their schedule.

win the battle. To beat the opponent.

win the pennant. To earn a championship in a given division of baseball.

win the pitch. Encouragement to a pitcher to concentrate on each pitch.

wipe the blood off that one. A term inferring that the hit was a bleeder.

wire-to-wire. When a team wins its division after being in first place every day of a season.

within their game. When a player plays within his limitations and abilities.

woody. Name for a wooden bat.

wore them out. Performed extremely well against a particular team.

work ahead. Phrase yelled to a pitcher encouraging him to get ahead in the count.

work hard. Encouragement given to a team to give their maximum effort.

workhorse. Term for 1) a player who plays hard and gives a club quality innings, or 2) a pitcher who throws a lot of innings for his team.

workload. The amount of pitching a pitcher does for a team.

work stoppage. A strike by the members of the Major League Baseball Player's Union or the Major League Baseball Umpire's Union.

w

work the count. When a hitter forces a pitcher to throw a lot of pitches in an at bat.

worm burner. Term for a pitch that hits the ground in front of the plate.

worst job in baseball. Expression some people use to describe a triple-A team manager's job.

WP. Abbreviation for wild pitches and winning pitcher.

WPCT. Abbreviation for winning percentage.

WS. Abbreviation for the Major League Baseball World Series.

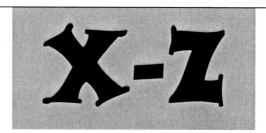

XBH. Abbreviation for extra base hits.

yacker. A great curveball.

yanked. Term for when 1) a pitcher is taken out of a game, or 2) a ball is pulled hard.

yard. Term for 1) a baseball field, or 2) a home run.

yard job. A home run.

yellow hammer. Slang for a great overhand curveball.

yellow snapdragon. A great curveball.

yeoman's job. A superb effort turned in by a player.

yes he did. Decision yelled by a base umpire after the plate umpire asks for help on a check swing.

yes he will. Warning yelled to the third baseman to tell him that the hitter will drag bunt.

yo yo. A player who is called up and sent down a few times in a season.

Yogism. Term for the famous sayings by the Yankees' great Yogi Berra.

you can't hide him. A saying that means if a team is trying to hide a poor fielder the ball will find him anyway.

you can't hit what you can't see. Expression yelled to imply that the pitcher is throwing so hard that the opposing batters can't see the pitches to hit.

W
X
Y
Z

you go, we go. Term of encouragement said to the player who is the team's catalyst meaning that if he gets on base the team will usually score a run.

you gotta dig. Encouragement yelled at a player that he has to run hard.

you hang 'em...we bang em. A phrase yelled by young players at an opposing pitcher telling him what they will do if he hangs a curveball.

you're due. Encouragement yelled at a batter to break out of a slump.

you're killin' us blue. Phrase yelled at umpires when a player, coach, or fan thinks they are doing a poor job.

you the man. Encouragement used to tell a player that he is important to the team in this situation.

you the one. Encouragement used to tell a player that he is important to the team in this situation.

zip on the ball. Velocity on the ball.

ANSWERS TO THE "DEFINE-THE-TERM" QUIZ PICTURES:

QUIZ

#1. (page 11) battery

#2. (page 20) big fly

#3. (page 20) bird dog scout

#4. (page 32) kick yer dog blue

#5. (page 39) bow yer neck

#6. (page 39) can of corn

#7. (page 51) captain hook

#8. (page 55) chin music

#9. (page 57) circus catch

#10. (page 57) come out of your shoes

#11. (page 60) doctor the bat

#12. (page 63) game face

#13. (page 66) gorilla ball

#14. (page 66) hole in his swing

#15. (page 76) pumpin' gas

#16. (page 81) right through the wickets

#17. (page 92) screamer

#18. (page 92) step in the bucket

#19. (page 102) wear the collar

#20. (page 102) wear the horns

Y
Z

Ryan Gray has been a part of successful baseball experiences his entire life. A native of Eldorado, Illinois, he was a member of the Eldorado High School baseball teams that played in three straight state playoffs. Gray was named to the first-team state tournament squad twice during those years. In 1984 his American Legion team from Harrisburg, Illinois competed in the Illinois State Championships. As a 1985 high school senior, Ryan was named the Southern Illinois Player of the Year.

Gray continued to play baseball after high school, joining two highly successful college programs. He played two years at Southeastern Illinois College in Harrisburg, Illinois and then the following two seasons at Union University in Jackson, Tennessee, where he was the second leading hitter on the Bulldogs' 1988 Tennessee Collegiate Athletic Conference championship club.

After coaching at the high school level for three years, he joined the coaching staff at Middle Tennessee State University as an assistant coach. In both of his seasons at MTSU, the Blue Raiders earned championship rings, and the 1995 squad played in the NCAA Division One Western Regional in Fresno, California. Gray then served as the head coach at Trevecca Nazarene University, where he coached two players who were selected as back-to-back Player of the Year (2000 and 2001) in the prestigious TranSouth Athletic Conference. Both are currently in professional baseball.

Gray is currently a scout for the Houston Astros. In 1995 he earned a doctoral degree at MTSU in Physical Education. He is married to the former Danica Colyer of Dexter, MO. They have two daughters, Reagan Danielle and Rylee Kate. The author currently resides in Nashville, Tennessee.